GUN CONTROL WILL WORK

JUST LIKE;

DRUG CONTROL

CRIME CONTROL

MIND CONTROL

&

PROHIBITION DID.

TO BELIEVE OTHERWISE
IS
THE HALLMARK
OF A FOOL

The Right to Keep and Bear Arms

America's Backbone

By Steven L. Kooyers, DC

ISBN-13: 978-1469948607

ISBN-10: 1469948605

ISBN-13#

ISBN-10 / EAN#

For information contact:

stevenkooyers200@gmail.com

"…the very atmosphere of firearms anywhere restrains evil interference - - they deserve a place of honor with all that's good."

George Washington

DISCLAIMERS

This book is NOT intended to be a reference work, but rather a source of motivation.

I tried, but couldn't authenticate any of the pasted quotations; however, they are seen in many different electronic media and websites, so I assume they're accurate or at least commonly attributed to whoever said them.

Here's one that's core to my theme...

"...let us carry ourselves back to the time when the Constitution was adopted, recollect the spirit manifested in the debates, and instead of trying what meaning may be squeezed out of the text, or invented against it, conform to the probable one in which it was passed."
Thomas Jefferson, letter to William Johnson
June 12, 1823, The Complete Jefferson, p322.

He was talking about those losers who look for loopholes, who ignore the spirit of the Bill of Rights.

The gun grabbers want you to believe they're for freedom... EXCEPT the freedom to own a gun. Perhaps they believe in irony, 'cuz they sure as hell don't believe in freedom.

Oh, wait; I'm getting ahead of myself. This is supposed to be the disclaimer section. Let's see if I got 'em all covered; most of the quotes came from the Internet, without verification. Don't do anything stupid.

Read these words in the spirit in which they were drafted. Yep, that's about it.

One last disclaimer; wherever I used derogatory words such as; moron, idiot, loser or dolt, you can be sure that I COULD HAVE chosen politically correct terms to give our gun-grabbing opponents more dignity... But when was the last time they *gave US dignity?*

Fellow gun-owners, it's time to fight fire with fire.

Contents

To FREEDOM

And to those
who purchased it for us
with their blood, guts and LIVES.
May we forever honor their sacrifice
by preserving and protecting
our precious freedom
for us, our kids,
and theirs
and...

"When they took the 4th Amendment,
I was quiet because I didn't deal drugs.

When they took the 6th Amendment,
I was quiet because I am innocent.

When they took the 2nd Amendment,
I was quiet because I don't own a gun.

Now they have taken the 1st Amendment,
and I can only be quiet."

attributed to Lyle Myhur

INTRODUCTION

When I was five, I got my first gun; a worn-out Daisy Cub, reclaimed from my neighbor's trash can. The stock was busted off, the front blade sight was bent, and the lever didn't lock into is holder... But it was a gun, by golly and *it was MINE!*

We lived in the country, 15 miles south of San Jose, California. Almaden was very rural; we were surrounded by fields and orchards; an outdoors mecca. And for BB gun toters? Mecca didn't come close to describing it.

If I wanted to see ducks, blackbirds, magpies or blue jays, all I had to do was look up or to the nearest field. The biomass was unbelievable. To make it even better, the nearest pond was only a mile away, chock-full of bluegills, dragonflies and bullfrogs.

I was too weak to cock the gun; had to have my mother cock it. The drawback was obvious; every time I shot I'd have to trudge home to reload. You already know how hit or miss the old BB guns were. Coupling the two pitfalls together, you can see my problem. My mom was Norwegian; tightwads in the extreme. So with each miss I'd get a little lecture on how expensive BB's were, and how we should eat what we finally kill. (If it ever happened)

I don't like lectures, so I was forced to develop two lifelong traits; improve my aim and get strong enough to cock my own rifle before my buddies discovered that momma had to cock my gun for me. If you shoot with both eyes open, your left eye can watch the BB fly, while maintaining the sight picture with your right. The images juxtapose. Then you can replay the miss all the way home. Get it cocked, *Go find another critter.* By the time I could cock the gun I acquired the habit of shooting with both eyes open, which has accounted for some spectacular shots that wouldn't be possible with one-eyed shooting.

After I wore out the Cub, my older siblings and Mom took pity and bought me a real gun; a daisy pump! From that point on, no bird or lizard was safe. The spring-driven magazine was a big improvement over the Cub's shake rattle & hope system.

By the time my friends, Louie, Joe and Donnie had 22's, we'd roam far and wide, routinely shooting birds on the wing and rabbits on the run. We learned how much to lead a running ground squirrel at eighty yards or a sprinting jackrabbit at fifty; We just felt it, knowing where he'd be at the zenith of a hop, and when the tiny projectile needed to be at that same spot. We were pretty awesome. But although I thought I knew everything about guns and hunting, I hadn't had a single lesson on the right to keep and bear arms; when the time was right, as usual, it was Mom that taught it.

Mom babysat for a woman newly moved into the first tract-home in the area. (Don't get me started on urban sprawl). Gay and Mom were sipping coffee when Louie, Joe and I entered the kitchen, covered in tarweed oil, squirrel blood and fish guts. As usual, we were armed to the teeth.

Gay saw the guns. She gasped in horror;
**"OH, CAROL! Did you KNOW
these children went out <u>WITH GUNS?</u>"**

Mom immediately retorted;
"Oh, <u>I wouldn't let 'em go WITHOUT 'em</u>."

The newest yuppie in south San Jose put her finger to her pursed lips. Then she quietly said;

"Oh, I see what you mean."

But we already knew the secret; there was a pervert living out there in the woods. What he did to young boys, nobody wanted done. So, yeah, we packed heat, long before it was considered cool. And the pervert? He found softer marks closer to the big city, where teens didn't carry lethal deterrents; so began my insight into why we keep and bear arms.

So, *THANKS AGAIN,* Mom. I miss you.

CH .177

SHOOTING LESSONS
WHAT IS THE SECOND AMENDMENT *REALLY ABOUT?*

"A free people ought not only to be armed and disciplined, but they should have sufficient arms and ammunition to maintain a status of independence from any who might attempt to abuse them, which would include

their own government."

George Washington

LESSON A;
IT'S *NOT ABOUT HUNTING!*

Some non-gunners say; "I MIGHT support having guns for hunting... *but not to carry!"* We should never sucker for this trap. The right to keep and bear is NOT about hunting, plinking, target practice or blasting rats in the basement.

Here's a news flash...

IT _NEVER WAS_ ABOUT HUNTING!

Read the 2nd Amendment. Do you see 'hunting' mentioned? Did the founders scribe the words; deer hunting? Ducks? Bwasted Wabbits?

The 2nd amendment was penned to give average citizens the ability to protect his self, family, property and country... *PERIOD.*

You need a LICENSE to hunt, since hunting is a PRIVILEGE.

BUT you don't need a license to speak freely,

to vote, to worship, etc...

But this doesn't stop the anti-hunters and anti-gun idiots from trying to get us to step onto this flypaper trap, where they can pluck off our wings and watch us squirm.

They want the issue clouded, because

that's the only way they can win.

If they can convince everyone that it's about hunting, they will win two big points; first, you don't need pistols or revolvers for hunting. This makes it simpler to ban those types of weapons.

Secondly, you won't need a gun after hunting season closes. So they'll insist that you store it at the police station until next season. Then, when they succeed in banning hunting, well... Can you see where the anti-gunners are headed? One need only watch the news to see how often city administrations yield to social pressure. OR to see how delighted most cops would be, if no citizens had any weapons.

In some countries, people can hunt with a variety of lesser implements; bow, crossbow, spear, air rifle, falcon or eagle. If we allow them to FOG the issue so that it were just about hunting, then say goodbye to our guns. (and once the guns are gone, say goodbye to hunting of any kind.)

SO IF IT'S NOT ABOUT HUNTING,
WHAT'S IT REALLY ABOUT?

For the real answer, let's look to the spirit of the bill; the revolutionaries had just thrown off the shackles of a tyrannical government. They needed every citizen to keep and bear arms, to stand ready to resist tyranny by ANY government, including the one they had just formed.

If you doubt me, then I suggest that you read Ben Franklin's discourse against having a standing army. The founders had seen standing armies go out of control and overthrow other nations where the People could not bear arms. Only the militia stood between standing armies and tyranny. Hence the precise wording of the second-amendment, where the distinction is made...

"A well regulated Militia, being necessary to the security of a free State, the right of the People to keep and bear Arms, shall not be infringed."

(J. Madison, T. Jefferson, et al)

They could have chosen any term, but they chose 'militia'. They could have drafted a bill to create a standing army, too, but *did they?* No. Can you blame them? When we see the founders' unbridled passion for liberty, there's no other conclusion possible...

THE 2ND AMENDMENT WAS
WRITTEN TO KEEP US FREE

LESSON B;
IT'S *NOT ABOUT HANDGUNS*

"A fear of weapons is a sign of retarded sexual and emotional immaturity."

Sigmund Freud

Gun-control freaks try to convince us that we don't need handguns because the 'militia' didn't use 'em. **What a crock!** Does the Second Amendment mention pistols? Shotguns? Rifles? How 'bout swords, nun-chuks or machetes?

The anti-gunners want everyone to think of handguns as sinister things, made only for criminals. Watch an hour of PRIMETIME TV to see how often they portray handguns as evil. Recall a certain movie scene (Lethal Weapon) where Mel Gibson decides to inspect his piece while inside the new precinct.

Danny Glover hollers; *'GUN!'* and tackles Mel. The room is crammed with other guys carrying guns, but that doesn't bother Glover at all. Ergo, Hollywood wants us to think that the ONLY BAD handguns are those that the cops don't own.

ARE HANDGUNS *BAD?*

If handguns are inherently evil, why are they one of the perks of command? U.S. Grant, Patton, Mcarthur; you name 'em; they all packed pistols.

The Hollywood anti-gun dolts love to conceal the fact that

good things are often achieved with pistols.

They certainly have a "let them eat cake" attitude regarding handguns. If you surf the internet you'll find lists of anti-gun celebs who are HYPOCRITICALLY packing heat.

Don't let 'em pull the wool over our eyes; the pistol is their "entry level drug". If they can divide us on handguns, we'll ultimately lose all of our guns.

That's what makes me so nervous; hunters are ALREADY making divisive statements; muzzle loaders criticize archers. Bowhunters criticize rifle hunters. Another group chastises tree-stand hunters or hunting over bait or with dogs. Flyfishermen ridicule worm fishing... and so on.

Divisiveness is counterproductive.

We're all blood brothers. Let's act like it...

While there's still time.

MOST DEFINITELY,

the second amendment

is NOT about handguns!

LESSON C;
IT'S *NOT ABOUT FLINTLOCKS*

One of the most THREADBARE arguments the brain-dead Hollywood types cling to is that We the People should be restricted to single-fire, slow-loading front-stuffers because that's what the colonialists used.

Their reasoning is flawed.

The Founders specified "arms" not muskets... What were these arms? State of the art, that's for sure! Muskets, pistols, mortars, cannons, fighting ships, you name it... If they could make it, buy it or steal it, they bore it against the King. Go to any reputable gun museum to see the types of arms they used; the variety is staggering.

American patriots have always had a love affair with state-of-the-art arms. They always wanted to upgrade; when the Second Amendment was penned, the People *WERE using state of the art weapons!* Furthermore, when percussion caps were invented, We the People converted flintlocks to percussion. Again, when cartridge cases were invented, We dropped the muzzle loader like a bad habit. And again, during the Civil War, We upgraded to repeaters.

Then later, We the People dropped our repeaters and bought semi-automatics. Do you see my point? Americans have always demanded and born... state of the art guns. And, God willing, we always will.

It's no accident that the 2nd Amendment specifically DOES NOT describe or limit the types of arms that the People were entitled to bear.

WHAT ELSE would the "well regulated militia"

expect to bear against tyrants,

the poorest guns?

If you consider that these rights were spelled out just after we waged war against Britain, and that the founding fathers were adamant that the People SHOULD BEAR ARMS against the government (if it got out of hand) then we must deduce that the People ought to bear arms of equal quality to the ones used by government. That is; flintlocks then, assault rifles now.

The SPIRIT in which the Bill of Rights was written compels us to make NO OTHER conclusion.

Trust me;

It's _not about FLINTLOCKS!_

LESSON D;
IT'S *NOT ABOUT MORE LAWS*

"Strict gun laws are about as effective as strict drug laws... It pains me to say this, but the NRA seems to be right: The cities and states that have the toughest gun laws have the most murder and mayhem." (Mike Royko, Chicago Tribune)

The gun-grabbers claim that laws prevent crime. What a crock! We have laws against rape and robbery, yet these occur with startling regularity.

When President Reagan was asked to sign another gun bill, he had aides bring out several bankers' boxes full of existing gun laws. He dropped one huge bill onto the podium with a resounding thump. He said something like; "We have over 3700 gun laws already; do we really need another one?"

Now, memory plays tricks on me; the number of laws might be wrong, but Ronnie's sentiments were spot-on. We don't need more laws, any more than starving people need more forks. Whenever I hear some dolt plead for more gun laws, I just want to bitch-slap some sense into the idiot.

Laws NEVER stopped crime and never will.

Why don't these gun-fearing morons advocate harsher penalties, more jail time and less plea bargaining for violent offenders when they break EXISTING laws?

I recall when the NRA-ILA supported legislation that would add 25 years for committing a felony with a gun. This seemed perfectly logical. We want crooks off the streets. And yet,

The press vilified the NRA

for its PRO-LAW ENFORCEMENT position.

How could any responsible newscaster be against such a law, which would punish only the convicted, violent criminals? Hollywood and the media forced me to one conclusion.

The gun grabbers just don't care

about law & order.

They just want our guns.

IT'S NOT ABOUT MORE LAWS!

LESSON E;
*IT'S ABOUT **FREEDOM***

The anti-gun dolts love to cloak their attack in sheep's clothing. They say *'it's not the Old West any more; you don't need guns.'* They'll lather it in guilt; they'll try to make you look bad, if you're a hunter, trapper, angler, farmer or other "bloodthirsty type" who exploits animals like all other societies have done since the beginning of time. They'll say whatever it takes to paint us as mouth-breathing slobs, too stupid to form coherent opinions.

But whatever they say,

one thing's certain;

they're ONLY after our freedom

If the subject happens to be; freedom of speech or the right to remain silent, they'll say that "The People" means us all, but they attack the 2nd Amendment as if the Devil wrote it; they'll say that The People means the army. How hypocritical. *How immoral!*

Perhaps the only thing worse is that we

have allowed such insane rhetoric

to go unchallenged.

It is patently absurd to think
that any of the first ten amendments
were out of synch with
the spirit of the others.
DON'T TRUST *ANYONE*
who messes with civil rights*!*

*"Guard with jealous attention
the public liberty.*

*Suspect everyone who
approaches that jewel.*

*Unfortunately, nothing will
preserve it but downright force.*

*Whenever you give up that
force, you are ruined.... The
great object is that every man be
armed. Everyone who is able
might have a gun."*

Patrick Henry, speech of June 14 1788

LESSON F;
WILL COPS PROTECT YOU?

THIS ARGUMENT HAS FOUR FLAWS,
ANY OF WHICH CAN GET YOU KILLED.

FLAW #1: THE AVERAGE POLICE RESPONSE in major cities runs three to ten minutes. Not bad, considering; traffic, dispatch lag, number of cops & doughnut shops. Most violent criminal attacks are over in a minute. Most gunfights? Ten seconds, which means the fastest cops will arrive in time to toe-tag victims and take reports from survivors... Which will you be?

FLAW #2: WILL THE COPS COME?
Police can be reluctant to enter areas known to be dangerous. And, if the caller says that the perp is armed, that 911 response may be slower. So if you live in such a neighborhood, forget the anti-gunners' piteous rhetoric. the cops probably won't come. (And if they do, you might be the one getting beaten, tasered, cuffed and busted)

Ask any gay or lesbian person who has reported a rape. Ask a barrio brother if the cops are eager to help them. The only ones naive enough to believe so are celebs, members of the white majority or those in law enforcement. For the rest of us in the real world, living outside of gated communities, it's quite possible that the cops won't even show up.

FLAW #3:

WHO WILL PROTECT YOU *FROM the COPS?*

It doesn't happen often, thank God... But rarely, *law officers turn bad.* Recently I saw a court TV episode; a deputy had publicly threatened to kill a man and his brother. The TV commentators painted the defendants guilty, merely for owning assault rifles, even though they were used to STOP AN ASSAULT, not to cause one.

According to testimony, the brothers were standing on their porch. Their backs were to the street, as they chatted with buddies on a peaceful Saturday morning. Suddenly, bullets started flying, striking one buddy. The brothers ran inside, located their weapons and returned fire at the rapidly approaching squad car, which was still firing as it approached. The deputy got killed. His 'unnamed assailant escaped injury.

The defendants were acquitted, since the forensics team found the deputy's spent brass way out by the mailboxes, proving he shot first, without warning or identifying himself. Oh; and that 'unnamed assistant' riding shotgun was ex CIA. Apparently, the defendant was a whistle blower in some type of atomic energy coverup.

Admittedly, it's rare for cops to go bad. Almost all cops are honest, courageous people, doing a thankless job. In my mind that makes 'em HEROES! But my point is simple; Might there be more 'bad cop' attacks on people with 'attitude problems, when NOBODY can own a gun for protection?

I hope we never have to find out.

FLAW 4; WHAT HAPPENS
WHEN COPS GET OVERWHELMED?

I remember the Watts riots; police were outnumbered. They parked on the fringe of the riot, so it couldn't sprawl to the "better" part of L.A.

UN-ARMED MERCHANTS
watched helplessly, while
RIOTERS PILLAGED THEIR STORES.

MEAHWILE, ARMED MERCHANTS
repelled the looters without firing a shot

Again, during the Rodney King riots,
Shopkeepers used guns to repel assaults,
NOT to cause them.

"Those who hammer their guns into plowshares
will plow for those who do not."
Thomas Jefferson, 3rd Pres of the United States

LESSON G;
WILL *GOVERNMENT...*
PROTECT *YOU?*

On the surface, it sounds good, doesn't it? Too bad it's only skin-deep. I ask you to think for a moment; WHO is your government?

Do the following statements

reflect a *trustworthy government?*

"If I could have banned them all - 'Mr. and Mrs. America turn in your guns' - I would have!" Diane Feinstein

We must stop thinking of the individual and start thinking about what is best for society." (Hillary Clinton, 1993)

"We can't be so fixated on our desire to preserve the rights of ordinary Americans" (President Bill Clinton, USA Today, March 11, 1993, Page 2A)

Obviously, some of our leaders are no longer concerned with individual rights; we have a HUGE problem. My point? Most bureaucrats think guns are evil; give 'em half a chance, they'll eagerly rip them from our twitching fingers. CPS thinks having a gun in your house is BAD for a child's safety. If an adoption agency learns you're a gun-owner, you won't get to adopt a kid. So much for government sentiment on private gun ownership. Now let's look at government's "desire" to protect us.

Our government is designed

to protect the weak.

If you own a gun you're NOT WEAK! Ergo, you don't deserve any help. In fact, the opposite seems true. Government doesn't trust you.

But the bigger issue is...

HOW MUCH SHOULD YOU

TRUST THE GOVERNMENT?

Many of today's young people weren't alive to see some of the abuses UNCLE SAM has foisted upon U.S. Citizens in the past.

During World War II, it incarcerated thousands of Japanese-Americans. They didn't do anything wrong. There was no DUE PROCESS. Their only 'crime' was their Japanese lineage.

The feds BROKE thousands of treaties with Native Americans. A bumper sticker sums it up;

"Ask an Indian if you can trust the government"

Young readers might NOT know about the Tuskegee Airmen and their incredible combat record during WWII. They saved lives and aircraft every day... But when these heroes came home, their government wouldn't allow them to fly civilian planes, simply because of their race!

During the Tuskegee Experiment, our government lied and mis-treated African-American patients having STD's. These CITIZENS were given sterile water injections, while being told it was medicine. The doctors and staff were told this experiment would benefit society.

Again, in the late '50s, our government sprayed attenuated nerve gas from Midwestern skyscrapers, to assess the efficacy of the toxins.

Now, the younger readers might say; "Ah, THAT was ancient history. *OUR government* wouldn't do anything like that NOWADAYS!"

It's time to pull our youngsters' heads out of the sand. What about those prisoners we tortured in GITMO, in direct violation of international treaty? Or Ruby Ridge, WACO or the CIA's covert MK II, a chemical brainwashing plan, to create assassins; Our government did all that.

Or take the recent chem-trail cover-up; at first they denied it but now government is putting a spin on it; Geo-engineering, to respond to a futuristic drought. *Please...*

Big Brother IS spraying nanoparticles of aluminum, boron and mylar into the upper atmosphere, even though these chemicals are toxic to humans and wildlife. Suddenly as if by magic, high levels of aluminum in our air and watershed is OK, in spite of the Library of Medicine's collection of 2,000 studies showing aluminum's harmful effects.

Experts have advocated protection of the ozone layer, to restrict VOC's and to conserve fossil fuels; meanwhile they're aerializing megatons of highly TOXIC particulates into American airspace.

History has shown government's relentless militarization of scientific discoveries. It will only be a matter of time before those jets will be aerializing lethal components, once they know where their poisons will land, thanks to this target practice.

"Fathom the Hypocrisy of a Government that requires every citizen to prove they are insured... but not everyone must prove they are a citizen."
Ben Stein, attorney & celeb

The federal government will eagerly trample our civil rights, if we give them the smallest excuse. Now that the **Patriot Act is law, (what an oxymoron; we should get it repealed)** our government can spy on everything you do, read, say, write or text, without a warrant. By the time this book is published, they'll be spying on me too, although I've never had a parking ticket.

If the younger generations doubt me on this topic, I almost can't blame 'em; it's too painful to think about it. Perhaps they would, if they would have lived during the McCarthy hearings, which destroyed thousands of lives on a nationwide witch hunt for communists, gays and other 'subversives'. We wasted millions of tax dollars to ruin the lives of those who were merely suspected of being "pinko". Our government justified it, which only makes it scarier to freedom-lovers.

If you're comfortable relying on
***this type* of government to protect you,**
God help you. God help us all.

CURRENT WORLD AFFAIRS PROVE IT; POWER CORRUPTS!

" ... for it is a truth, which the experience of all ages has attested, that the people are commonly most in danger when the means of insuring their rights are in the possession of those of whom they entertain the least suspicion."

Alexander Hamilton

You don't have to look hard to see GOVERNMENT-sanctioned atrocities; Recently in Darfur, (the independent sultanate recently *incorporated* into Sudan) soldiers massacred non-Arab indigenous people, after beating and raping whomever they wanted.

Government-sponsored racial annihilation...

who would think we'd see it again,

after Hitler?

What did our president do, during this annihilation? He was busily bowing before the king of Saudi Arabia. (this footage leaked out of Israeli TV, since American TV wouldn't show it. I wonder ; would Barak have bowed to Hitler, too?)

LESSON H;
WILL OUR ARMY PROTECT US?

The anti-gunner would bet his Prius that we don't need guns, since our armies will protect us. But the gun-control dolts have it wrong again, as usual.

Praise the Lord, we do have great soldiers!

WE GOT 'EM <u>FROM</u>

OUR WELL REGULATED MILITIA

Scratch any U.S. sniper and you'll hear of a lifelong LOVE of firearms. Our snipers grew up shooting varmints, deer & birds. Then in Basic, someone noticed their home-grown talent and then supplied specialized training.

A concert violinist doesn't just BECOME excellent upon admission to Julliard; the fiddler's 'militia' began at home at a tender age. The innate skill was noticed, then later polished, just as the sniper's was. First came the talent, then the training.

Certainly we have a powerful military force. It's the strongest on earth. We couldn't survive without it. But to think that this negates our moral and patriotic responsibility to bear arms is not only simplistic, but downright foolhardy. History has shown the downfall of powerful nations occurred when they relied on standing armies alone.

But it's not just about front line warfare; IF times get rough during war (and they usually do) it's anyone's guess what the homeland scenario might morph into, but history has shown that you'll be left on your own. Who's going to protect you from your formerly nice neighbors? If you've never seen people fighting for air, water or life jackets, it ain't pretty.

To the younger readers, this subject might seem improbable. I'll ask you to look back in time, to the early 60's. The USSR began installing missiles in Cuba. Americans started building bomb shelters. Survivalists disagreed on which items you should store, but every pundit agreed that a gun be included, for the most primal reason of all; to keep neighbors from taking your food and last drop of non-nuked water.

From our affluent position, it seems preposterous. But imagine that you're weak and unarmed. Your bigger neighbor is kicking down your door. While you're wondering what you'd do, I can predict his actions; he will overpower you and take whatever he needs. He might even assault the females of your home; it's the law of the jungle.

"Trust your neighbor,
but brand your cattle"

Anti-gunners might say
'it can't happen here'
and I hope they're right...

I'm asking you to temporarily ignore terrorism, the middle east crisis, the black market sale of ICBMs & lost/stolen shipments of Plutonium, OK?

Our neighbors are far more likely to bake us a cake than to rob and rape us, but it certainly illustrates the baseness of mankind and how thin our facade really is. People already hurt each other in a spontaneous case of road rage or an argument over a parking space. Use your imagination; is it really THAT BIG A STRETCH, to think we'd kill each other over the last can of tuna?

"We're just apes
with baseball caps
and automatic weapons."
George Carlin

LESSON I;
FLIES DON'T *CAUSE* GARBAGE

Many gun-grabbers claim that handguns cause crime, since they're easy to conceal. And to be fair, it's pretty tough to sneak a side-by-side shotgun inside your hip pocket. But the anti-gunners miss real the point. OR perhaps they deliberately ignore the REAL FACTS that don't support their argument.

HANDGUNS ARE MEANT TO BE CONCEALED

Fertilizer is meant to feed plants.

Diesel is meant to fuel trucks.

Knives are meant to cut stuff.

Does that mean we are criminals if we own fertilizer, diesel or knives? I'll bet you own pistols, revolvers or a pair of black powder duelers, yet you've never committed a crime with them.

Whenever you start with the OUTCOME and backtrack to support your conclusion, that's called JUNK SCIENCE. I once read a study on crime; all of the inmates had eaten potatoes while growing up; ergo, potatoes cause crime. It's ludicrous, isn't it?

Potatoes don't make crooks.

Neither do guns.

The problem isn't handguns.

It's the twisted, immoral, self-serving slobs that rob people. These crooks would rather rob than work. They want to harm, not help. They take, instead of contribute. They just don't give a damn about society. When crime control is the goal, we must look at the criminal's impulse control disorder and how to cure it or alter it so it ceases to culminate in criminal acts.

And, when people ignore this key issue and choose instead to point their fingers at OUR guns, we must question their motivation.

A crook will always be a crook, until something inside his mind gets re-wired the correct way. Until that time, jail will have to suffice. But let's never forget that...

GUNS DON'T CAUSE CRIME
ANY MORE THAN
FLIES CAUSE GARBAGE

LESSON J;
GUNS DON'T KILL PEOPLE

Why would anyone make such an imbecilic statement? Maybe because they're imbeciles, I'm guessing. Certainly, you'd be a lunatic to deny that guns are made to kill, but there are INTENTIONAL steps to take before you can shoot anything.

STEP 1 Get gun. You'll need your "B vitamins;" Buy, Borrow, Beg, Burgle or Build a gun.

STEP 2 Get bullets. Most people won't stick around for 'death by pistol-whip'.

STEP 3 Learn to load. There are buttons and mag releases to find and press, in the right sequence.

STEP 4; Learn to shoot. Contrary to TV, it's easy to miss. You'll need to practice.

STEP 5; Get close. The last (TV) cop-cam shootout I saw had 1 cop, two bad guys and 41 shots fired in ten seconds. Only two bullets struck one bad guy, who survived.

STEP 6; Aim & pull trigger. This last step is every bit as INTENTIONAL as the prior ones are.

To shoot someone requires
DELIBERATE INTENTION.

It ISN'T THE GUN,
BUT
The *CRIMINAL MINDSET*
that's the taproot of all crime.

Every day in America, people murder others , using; knives, bats, golf clubs, rope, poison, drugs or bombs. When a person has criminal intent, there's no limit to the type of weapons to choose from. Homicides will continue to occur, as long as the criminal Intention is present,

LESSON K;
MEDICINE'S GUN BIAS

Most DOCTORS dislike guns. This sentiment runs strongest among docs who treat gunshot wounds. But it's not just guns; doctors are inherently prejudicial against all risk factors.

When I was young, a drunk driver hit me while I was riding a bicycle. He was an illegal alien with NO driver license or insurance and he blew 0.28; almost the fatal limit.

I thank God that my injuries were fairly small; MTBI, busted scapula, Trapiezius muscle lacerated to the bone, rt ear mostly cut off, and small contusions & cuts to face, throat, scalp. It could have been worse; I could have been killed.

The doctor was a beautiful, young, plastic surgery resident; she started tweezing glass shards, without anesthetic, since they were still assessing my brain injury. I tried to be tough, so I looked up into her gorgeous hazel eyes. When you're 19, that works *almost* as well as Novocaine. Every time the tweezers touched another shard, she'd mutter that clear glass should be outlawed...

**But not once did the doctor growl
about drunk driving,
which caused the man
to run me over.**

I healed up fine, but it taught me how doctors usally take the patient's side. Later, when my son went in for multiple scorpion stings, the doctor ranted about stinging critters... But he never asked AJ if he bothered to shake out his boots before lacing 'em up. Out west in most hunting camps, we do this every morning, but AJ hadn't. *Now?* He shakes those boots like a man possessed.

DOCTORS RARELY ACKNOWLEDGE THAT GUNS PREVENT CRIME & INJURIES

Consider what a psychiatrist could say to a patient that shot her assailant BEFORE he had the one-sided pleasure of becoming her rapist...

> *"How wonderful!*
> *You've come a long way,*
> *since your last rape!*
> *You're self-empowered!*
> *See you next Friday!"*

Her OB/GYN might say;
> *"Sara, I'm so glad you*
> *shot the bastard before he could*
> *give you STD's...*
> *or kill you!"*

I should emphasize that SOME DOCTORS do actually hunt, fish and handle guns responsibly. Too bad these docs are rarely the ones offering their opinions to the gun-grabbing bureaucrats and others who hold positions of influence.

CH .22

"But if someone has a gun and is trying to kill you...

it would be reasonable

to shoot back

with your own gun."

the Dalai Lama

Despite the Dalai Lama's keen advice, there still remains plenty of...

BAD LOGIC in the anti-gun camp.

Let's take a look at some of it, in this chapter.

BAD LOGIC; GUNS ARE EVIL

To counter this absurd statement, **you may wish to pose these questions:**

1. **DO YOU CHERISH FREEDOM?**
2. **DO YOU ABHOR SLAVERY?**
3. **DO YOU THINK OPPRESSION IS BAD?**
4. **SHOULD HITLER HAVE BEEN STOPPED?**
5. **ARE YOU AGAINST CRIME?**

If they answer 'yes' to one, you win! Guns freed us from tyranny, won the west, freed the slaves. Guns stopped Hitler, Mussolini & Stalin.

Guns stop crimes every day.

Guns in the hands of responsible citizens defend life, liberty and property on a daily basis. Guns for or Navy Seals brought Bin Laden to justice.

Around this point in the debate, the anti-gunner will switch tack; *"Oh, I didn't mean guns for war, I meant I'm against private gun ownership!'*

Now you can retort; private ownership of guns kept Japan from invading America in WWII and kept a genocidal maniac like Hitler Hitler from invading the Swiss, steadfastly locked & loaded high up in their mountains.

The anti-gunner may switch tack again,
saying something really stupid:

"OH, NOT <u>THOSE</u> GUNS!
I'M AGAINST THE CHEAP,
LOW QUALITY GUNS!"

ONLY an arrogant elitist would say that. These unimaginative hypocrites thrive on double standards and unequal protection. Only someone who's never been in DIRE need of a gun could make such a callous, egocentric statement while maintaining a straight face.

THEY ARE REALLY SAYING;
"I DON'T CARE ABOUT POOR FOLKS."

WELL, ALL I CAN SAY IS...
THREE CHEERS FOR
THE SATUDAY NIGHT SPECIAL!

(Turn the page!)

ENTER THE LIBERATOR!

During **Hitler's siege,** troops would roll into town and broadcast; all guns to be on the streets. A few rusty guns would clatter to the streets. The Nazis would search, find a gun, then haul the owner into the street; a bullet to the head came next. Soon Hitler had what he wanted; all civilian firearms, and the power to annihilate millions of unarmed people.

Something had to be done.

WE the People came up with a stopgap weapon, stamped out of sheet metal, with a pull-cock hammer. It was chambered in .45 ACP. Obviously, without any rifling, the Liberator couldn't hit squat beyond a few yards. But it was a gun, by God!

The plan was brilliantly simple: Air-drop thousands of Liberators into occupied Europe. When the citizens got the chance? Shoot a Nazi and take his superior guns.

More than one Nazi fell

to these Saturday Night Specials,

thus proving Cooper's rule...

"Remember the first rule of gunfighting; have a gun."

Col John Dean "Jeff" Cooper

May 10, 1920 - September 25, 2006

In reality, the OSS (which later became the CIA) didn't see the need, so fewer than the planned number of Liberators were actually deployed. But martial historians debate which was more effective; the Liberator or the psychological effect of knowing that pistols were in the hands of desperate people. But either way, cheap handguns played a role in saving countless millions of lives.

HEY! IT *DIDN'T END*
WITH THE LIBERATOR

During the U.S. early involvement in Vietnam there was a similar plan to inseminate the theater with cheap pistols. The CIA called it the "deer gun," Arguably the poorest code name for a spy gun, but what can I say; I didn't name it, they did.

Before they deployed many Deer Guns, the war escalated exponentially, which made the Deer Gun plan a moot point. Nonetheless, the plan clearly reflected the effectiveness of the earlier Liberator and its psychological effect upon the enemy.

So when you hear any jerk claim that there's no good reason for cheap handguns, you should challenge that argument. Either the moron hasn't thought it through OR is just an arrogant, self-absorbed slob, too lazy to research history or the plight of war-torn people. Either that or he/she hates poor people.

Thankfully, the good folks at the NRA actually do care about normal citizens. I recall an incident; (although there are thousands) it happened back in the nineties, if memory serves me. A boy was forced to shoot someone in self-defense. The defendant wasn't a hunter or NRA member. He lived in the 'hood; not exactly the typical scenario you might read about in the newspaper, is it?

Where in the Constitution

does it say that poor people

don't deserve civil rights?

The Prosecution called the defendant a vigilante, claiming his gun was for doing drive-bys, although the kid had a spotless record. He wasn't a gangster, but the <u>dead guy was</u>.

THANKS TO THE NRA,

THIS KID WAS ACQUITTED.

AMEN, *PASS THE AMMO!*

Gun-grabbing sensationalists argue that barrio buddies only use their pistolas to cause crime, but a recent estimate (gun-grabber website,@ 2012) said; Americans own 300 million guns, mostly in densely populated ghettos, barrios, 'hoods or whatever you call them. The bulk of these guns remain inside homes, quietly waiting to defend the occupants AGAINST *REAL* criminals, if they're unlucky enough to invade an armed home.

If guns really do cause crime,
Then we'd see much more crime
in these heavily armed barrios.
Perhaps it's because guns deter crime
in ghettos, just as they do
everywhere else.

God bless the NRA
for having the vision
and the gumption...
to take such a stand.

*"If guns cause crime,
MINE must be defective!"*

Ted Nugent

MORE BAD LOGIC IN THE ANTI-GUN HERD

"Gun control? It's the best thing you can do for crooks and gangsters.

I WANT you to have nothing...

I'm a bad guy;

I'm always gonna have a gun.

Safety locks?

You will pull the trigger

with a lock on

and I'll pull the trigger...

We'll see who wins."

Sammy The Bull Gravano

(whose testimony convicted John Gotti)

"False is the idea of utility that sacrifices a thousand real advantages for one imaginary or trifling inconvenience; that would take fire from men because it burns, and water because one may drown in it; that has no remedy for evils except destruction. The laws that forbid the carrying of arms are laws of such a nature. They disarm only those who are neither inclined nor determined to commit crimes."

(**Cesare Beccaria,** as quoted by Thomas Jefferson's Commonplace book)

**LET'S LOOK AT SOME OF
THE ANTI-GUNNER
RHETORIC.**

**For a few pages,
PLEASE humor me; melt down your guns,
along with your common sense;
let's"dummy down" and step into
the rubber coated world.**

HERE WE GO...

NO GUNS, *NO CRIME?*

Is there a better litmus for stupidity? This presumption is delusional and preposterous. Still, they cling to it, so we must destroy it.

**CLEARLY, GUN-FREE ZONES
ARE TARGETS FOR CRIME,
NOT HAVENS**

IF NO GUNS EQUALS NO CRIME,THERE
SHOULDN'T BE ANY CRIME
IN PRISON, RIGHT?

In spite of the ABSENCE OF GUNS, crimes occur in staggering numbers. It's very common for prisoners to fashion LETHAL WEAPONS from toothbrushes, spoons, wire, you name it! Murders, rapes, assault & full-blown riots occur in prisons, without guns!

Our critics might say; "Prison is a special circumstance; it doesn't count." Here's another...

GUNS AREN'T ALLOWED
IN HOSPITALS, EITHER

According to a recent airing of Sixty Minutes, patients are killed, raped, robbed, molested and assaulted right in the very room that's supposed to be safe. No guns, yet plenty of crime, RIGHT IN OUR HOSPITALS. They advocate having a guardian whenever you're in a hospital bed, a nursing facility or any other place where you're virtually helpless.

GUNS AREN'T ALLOWED
IN SCHOOLS...

In "gun-safe" school yards, our children are frequently bullied, molested, raped, abducted, stabbed & killed... Again, this refutes the 'no guns, no crime' hogwash THAT spews from morons. Personally, I find it reprehensible that teachers aren't allowed to pack heat, to protect our kids.

AIRPORTS ARE GUN-FREE ZONES

Ergo, one might expect airports and planes to be crime-free. And yet, while standing in line for a commercial flight, I scoped out a display board showing the various things the FAA considers to be "weapons"; aerosol cans, corkscrews, metal toothpicks, archery gear or fishing nooks. Crimes can be caused with all these weapons, and more.

NO GUNS, NO CRIME,
BUT *A STUBBORN ZINFANDEL?*

A dear friend told me of her flight from New Zealand; a corkscrew on her key chain was her good luck charm, and oh, so handy for a stubborn wine cork. The Kiwi security guard noticed it;
"Hey, what's this?"
"My lucky charm; I've had it for years!"
"Where are you headed?"
"San Francisco"
"OH, *THAT WON'T DO!*"

They confiscated her corkscrew, but once the plane got to cruising altitude, they served steaks. Each passenger got a metal serrated steak knife. Terri never got over that. But still, nobody hijacked the plane, in spite of all the "weapons."

"No matter how one approaches the figures, one is forced to the rather startling conclusion that the use of firearms in crime was very much less when there were no controls of any sort and when anyone, convicted criminal or lunatic, could buy any type of firearm without restriction. Half a century of strict controls on pistols has ended, perversely, with a far greater use of this weapon in crime than ever before."

Colin Greenwood, in study "Firearms Control" 1972

MORE BAD LOGIC; BANNING THE ELEMENTS OF CRIME WILL DETER IT?

This argument lies at the bottom of the mental sewer; anyone with a working brain can see through it, but WHO said anti-gunners have working brains?

Maybe this'll help.
Pardon my spoofs...

The NATIONAL COALITION to BAN SPOONS

"Hi, I'm Steve Kooyers, CEO of NCBS.

Spoons cause obesity, death & disease. Especially evil are high-capacity spoons, which allow people to eat more without reloading. Private citizens shouldn't own spoons, which are used to commit crimes against the body. If spoons were banned, obesity would vanish. Sure, they could still use forks, but they couldn't eat so much at one time. Just think; soups, bisque, gravies and broths fall right through forks. Help our country get lean.

JOIN US NOW...
LET'S outlaw spoons!

AMERICANS AGAINST SNAP-BLADE KNIVES

The AASK wants to ban snap-blades, known on the street as box cutters, the weapon of choice for suicide. Anyone can walk in a store and get this mass-produced weapon, whose only purpose is to kill.

There's no cooling-off period; an upset housewife can buy one, whenever she wants. Worse yet, the same store might also sell alcohol and drugs! There's no limit, either; I bought 100 knives in one store. Nobody even asked for my ID.

Help us end the suicides!

But it doesn't end with suicides; do you remember September 11, 2011? Terrorists killed three thousand people with snap blades!

AND YET, NOBODY HAS SPOKEN OUT AGAINST BOX-CUTTERS!

Which is why I founded the AASK

Help us outlaw this weapon of mass destruction before more terrorists hijack more planes and kill more Americans! Sure, it might inconvenience many people, but it will be worth it if we can keep one person from being a terrorist.

To paraphrase Sara Brady:
I don't believe box-cutter owners have any rights.

FARMERS AGAINST AMMONIUM NITRATE

Hi, I'm the founder of FAAN... One day I went out to fertilize my crops, but my tank was mysteriously empty. I called the sheriff, who said; *"Steve, you're the FIFTH farmer to lose fertilizer this week! I don't know where it's going!"*

The next day, we found out... A federal building full of people was blown to bits.

SO, I founded the FAAN
HELP us ban fertilizer!

Who cares, if America doesn't grow as much food? It would be worth it, if we can keep one poor, disturbed youth... from becoming a bomber.

DON'T LET FERTILZER
TURN PEOPLE INTO CRIMINALS!

ANTI RAPE COALITION

We can end rape
with just a few new laws

➢ **BAN FEMALES FROM TRAVELING.** Many rapes happen when women travel.

➢ **BAN ATTRACTIVE CLOTHES & FLIRTING.** Females shouldn't wear things that trigger the urge to rape. Neither should they strut or flirt wherever men are LIKELY to be.

➢ **HIRE MORE COPS.** A cop in every bedroom could eliminate date rape & spouse rape.

➢ **FIRE ALL WOMEN.** 30% of all rapes occur in the workplace.

➢ **REDUCE FEMALE POPULATION;** a touchy subject, but less females means fewer rapes.

➢ **TAGGANTS ON ALL FEMALES.** Inject girls with RFID chips, so cops will always know where women are.

Controversial? Fewer civil rights?
Sure, but it would be WORTH IT,
to prevent just one rape!
JOIN ARC NOW!

Citizens Against Assault Dogs

The Pit Bull, the Doberman Pincher, Rotweiler and German Shepherd are bred to be assault dogs. If we BAN fighting breeds we could end all pit fights!

These dogs and their breeders are ALREADY REGISTERED in each county. We could seize the lists, confiscate the dogs and arrest the breeders. Make it a felony to breed, sell or own assault-dogs.

I know what you're thinking; these criminals might start fighting smaller dogs. They would put spaniels or poodles in the pit fights. Don't worry; we'll get the smaller dogs later. The streets will be safe again, once all the breeders & trainers are in jail.

END DOG VIOLENCE...
JOIN THE CAAD TODAY!

As soon as I get enough federal funding, I'm going to start some MORE orgs, too. I shall...

BAN ALL RENTAL TRUCKS & VANS!

Remember the FIRST World Trade Center attack AND Oklahoma City? The bombers packed rental trucks with explosives. WHEN we destroy these tools of mass destruction, terrorists couldn't bomb us. Help me ban rental trucks!

BAN GO-FAST BOATS!

STEALTH & GO-FAST BOATS ARE ONLY FOR SMUGGLING DRUGS. Let's ban them; (of course the boat racers will complain, but they're just a small community; nobody will rally to their cause.)

BAN PRIVATE AIRCRAFT

No private planes, no air-dropped drugs... Simple!

BAN INTERNATIONAL TRAVEL

If coke can't get here, we can't have a coke problem.

BAN TIRE IRONS & LUG WRENCHES

Plenty of thugs use 'em to commit crimes. If we eliminate the iron, crime will go away.

OK, BEFORE YOU SKIN ME ALIVE...

I'm not against women, dogs, trucks or fertilizer. And as for SPOONS, I have an arsenal of high-capacity spoons locked in my gun safe. But can you see the common thread? These sham arguments address the implement, instead of the criminals who use them to commit crimes.

**SO WHEN SOMEONE STARTS
SPEWING THE
"NO-GUNS, NO-CRIMES" RHETORIC,
LET 'EM HAVE IT
RIGHT BETWEEN THE EYES
WITH YOUR FAVORITE
SNAPPY COMEBACK**

**Do WRENCHES make a mechanic crooked?
Does a SAW make a contractor a cheat?
Do PULPITS turn priests into pedophiles?
Do MATCHES create arsonists?
Do TIGHT SKIRTS cause rapists?
Do pretty cars create car thieves?**

Cops often plant gorgeous "sting cars." But do they catch law-abiding people? How many sweet cars do you walk by in a parking lot? Do YOU steal them? No; you're not a criminal.

**IT IS TOTALLY IRRATIONAL
TO BLAME THE TOOL OR THE VICTIM
FOR THE CRIMINAL'S ACTION**

**Until we face the fact
that the REAL problem
is the criminal mind,
Crime will still be high.**

Americans currently own @ 350 million guns. If guns cause crime, then we ought to see the highest crime in areas with the most guns. And yet, time and again, we see the opposite,. Chicago, Washington DC and other gun-phobic cities have the highest crime, while pro-gun bergs have the lowest.
(I urge you to surf justfacts)

"Strict gun laws are

about as effective

as strict drug laws...

It pains me to say this,

but the NRA seems to be right:

The cities and states

*that have the toughest gun laws
have the most murder and
mayhem."*

Mike Royko, Chicago Tribune

CH .243

HOW DO WE FIX IT?

"... Our Constitution
was made only for a
moral and religious people.
It is wholly inadequate
to the government
of any other."
John Adams

*"There are
hundreds of millions
of gun owners
in this country,
and not one of them
will have an accident today.
The only misuse of guns
comes in environments
where there are drugs, alcohol,
bad parents and
undisciplined children...Period."*
Ted Nugent, rock n roll icon,
freedom activist

Anti-gunners might say; *'take all the guns, melt them into plowshares; our problems will be over.'* Meanwhile, we gun-lovers want more guns so we can protect ourselves from the zombies.

I'm sure that nobody really thinks the gun debate is as simple as this or that the problem is really about guns; wise people know better than that.

But wherever you stand on the issue, you must admit that our society has fundamental problems that go much deeper than guns. Until these are rectified we shall continue to have high recidivism rates and way too much violence.

Until we take certain steps, our insanely high crime rate won't get any lower. The following pages have a few steps that I think we need to take.

PUT GOD
FRONT & CENTER AGAIN

"Train up a child in the way he should go: and when he is old,

he will not depart from it"

Proverbs 22:6, KJV Bible

We desperately need the morals which made this country great. No country can prosper for very long, without ethics. History proves it, over and over.

It's great to take children fishing & hunting, but take 'em to church too. We desperately need to restore faith in God. Think back; when was the last time a Christian hijacked a plane or built a weapon of mass destruction? Given the media's overt prejudice against Christianity, they would certainly highlight it, so you would've heard about it.

But the facts speak for themselves; children in homes that fear the Lord are NEVER the problem. They are the solution. Faith-based societies have less crime, less drug abuse and less divorce.

When children grow up with proper values, they pass them down to their children. That preserves our country. It's time we stopped apologizing for our faith. Time to promote it, actually.

"Evil prospers when good men do nothing"

What the a-moralists have done with our country is practically criminal, but perhaps what's worse is that we let 'em get away with it.

Christianity has come under vicious attack, while other religions have been cultivated. While the atheists were busy getting the Ten Commandments pulled from some southern courthouse, Barack Hussein was trying to put a Mosque at Ground Zero in NYC. And, since the media failed to criticize him for this OBVIOUS and ILLEGAL mixture of church & state, it seems that only Christianity is in the Fed's cross-hairs.

Perhaps we Christians have been way too busy turning the other cheek. Our nation's schools got into the morals game, under the guise of church/state cleansing. Predictably, the results are abysmal. Fifth-graders aren't being taught to abstain or have any moral compunction whatsoever. Instead, they're taught to put condoms on bananas. While the intent was to reduce STD's and pregnancies, (which was partially effective; teen preg rate halved, from '76-'06) our state-sponsored surrogate parents (translate; teachers) send the message that it's OK to have safe sex.

But every decent parent knows; there's no such thing as safe sex when children are having it.

Yet in spite of a barrage of

compulsory videos, pamphlets, counseling,

sex-ed classes and available birth control

for children too young to shave,

the national under-14 pregnancy rate

hovers at 8:1000.

The state's best effort

to rear our children

rates an F.

Faith-based schools aren't perfect, but they work better than public schools

If we were to compare our public schools to faith-based schools, you'd be shocked. While our kids are "hooking up" for promiscuous sex, getting pregnant and transmitting STDs, the Buddhist schools (separation of sexes through high school) have few sexual issues. I bet it's the same for most other faith-based schools, which have stood the test of time, while our public schools steadily spiral out of control. What a pity that our government-sponsored educators 'know better'.

Virtually every problem that our schools now face are self-inflicted. Furthermore, until we reinstate worship and moral values, these problems will continue to exacerbate.

TEACH GUN SAFETY TO ALL!
FIREARMS ARE INHERENTLY DANGEROUS

So are; knives, gasoline, table saws, chainsaws, cars and motorcycles, yet it doesn't stop teachers from teaching kids how to safely use these items. Why shouldn't we teach kids how to safely use firearms? It's irresponsible not to teach this.

Recently I watched a drunken idiot on TV; he stumbled around with beer and a shotgun. He fired it, then the recoil kicked him down a hillside. His buddies laughed. The narrator was quick to say that no one got hurt, but it seemed like an endorsement of horrid gun-handling technique. Obviously, we should never drink alcohol while using firearms. To air such a spot is immoral. Kids mimic what they see on TV.

We should do whatever we can, to promote responsible gun handling, on television as well as in person. Most firearms teachers try to instill a mindset of RESPECT, since that's the foundation for safety.

Sadly, RESPECT is sorely lacking in today's younger generations. Trash-talking is at an all-time high. Impulsive actions dominate young people, who rarely consider how those impulses affect others. These kids need the mental focus and clarity that gun-safety courses usually instill in most of the students.

RESTORE THE FAMILY UNIT

Many of today's 'parents' don't merit the term. From trailer-trash rednecks who shoot at power lines while their wives fill Baby's bottle with Pepsi, to affluent double income couples swilling martinis, America's parenting skills have never been worse.

IDLE HANDS; THE DEVIL'S WORKSHOP

The recent epidemic of schoolyard shootings have shown it; the perps are almost always from affluent homes. None of them held jobs, did chores or worshiped the Lord. Their parents gave them the best of everything; allowances, long hours playing video games and generally being worthless. The parents thought they were doing the best for their children by coddling them.

WHEN WILL WE EVER LEARN?

Recently, a fact-based re-enactment aired on cable TV; a group of youths with plenty of free time & money, no supervision, chores or jobs spent their hours getting wasted and having sex. Their parents didn't care enough to check on them. Instead, they chose to float down the river of denial. Funny thing about about floating; you can ONLY GO DOWNHILL. It wasn't long before the old adage proved true; the youths killed their leader of their gang. When cops arrested them, none of them realized that they'd committed a serious crime. One defendant said; *"Oh, sure, we killed him but it wasn't like we MURDERED him or anything."*

So much for giving kids everything.

RESTORE ACCOUNTABILITY

Out here in California, we avoid accountability as if it were the Plague. Recently, a local newspaper called a gun-death an *accident.* They tacked on the word "tragic" to soften the blow. But ALTHOUGH it was tragic, it wasn't an accident. It was so avoidable, I'm surprised the sheriff didn't arrest anybody.

The family went out to cut firewood. They had dogs, guns, chainsaws and kids. And beer. The kids carried wood to the trucks. When finished working, they started shooting beer & pop cans. Later, the youngest boy got into the truck with a .LOADED 22. He dropped it. Rifle fired. Bullet nicked his femoral artery. At first, they thought it was a lucky miss. The boy bled out right there in the truck, before his drunken parents knew what hit him.

If you put loaded guns, alcohol and kids in a vehicle, something's going to go bang... That's not an accident, it's a prediction... And a helluva bad bad way to train kids.

When we lead a life of vice and excess, our kids will grow into worthless idiots who think that every bad thing is an accident; it's an ACCIDENT that your daughter got knocked up at a rave. It's bad luck that your alcoholic son didn't get hired for a great job. It's an accident that your wife died of an overdose. It's all bad luck.

Actually, it's all about choices.

I never still-hunt with a round chambered in my rifle. Twice I fell down hard enough that the gun *could have* discharged, if it had been loaded.

My wife & kids hunt the same way, without so much as a cut finger. Sure we slip and fall; if you hunt rugged terrain, that's going to happen, but those rifles have empty throats until we're ready to shoot a critter.

If you teach kids with love, respect and courtesy, there's no place for accidents to take root. That is the seed-core of the Well Regulated Militia; respectful families who teach responsibility to others.

**"A militia,
when properly formed,
are in fact
the people themselves ...
and include all men
capable of bearing arms."**
Richard Henry Lee

TAKE KIDS SHOOTING & FISHING

I believe in teaching children according to their level of maturation. When kids earn respect, they give it back. When they learn discipline and safety, the thing snowballs. Once we reach critical mass, our society will improve drastically.

However, when adults paint the world as a peaceful, warm and fuzzy place, it's no wonder that some children reject this lie, then turn to violence. But show a video of a Great White Shark munching on a squealing seal and you have their full attention. Why not prepare our kids for reality? Kids are passionately honest. They deserve the truth. It's a dog eat dog world out there.

When I take a child fishing, I start with food chain basics. We find minnows, because bigger fish will be eating them. That's how the whole world works, and everybody knows it. (except some teachers) The child always gets it on the first take.

We take a few fish home. It empowers them to see their rightful role *as a predator* and a provider. Sure, there's plenty of time later to teach catch 'n release, but in the meantime, a few filets go a long way toward creating a lifelong enthusiast. My six year-old grandson already has trout, bluegills, smallies and large-mouth bass to his credit. I've never seen a kid so fired up about outdoor sports. Hopefully you'll have some fanatics, too... But don't stop with just your kids. Take neighborhood children, too.

TAKE 'EM OUTSIDE!

Our kids spend WAY too much time playing mind-warping video games and texting their shallow-breathing peers, instead of hoofing all over our great country. It's a dangerous society that teaches children that all pleasure and satisfaction should be derived from electronic media. It's a mistake to let kids live and play continually in 'the land of delete' where errors have no real consequence. To do so is to cultivate the seeds of national destruction.

How can we teach ecology and resource management to children that won't get off the couch? How are such children going to sustain a way of life that was earned with sweat, blood and sacrifice?

When the next ballot proposes another strip mall in that old swampy spot, which of these children will vote for the Wood Ducks, Salamanders and Egrets, if all they know is electronic pleasure?

TAKE 'EM OUTDOORS!

If certain children don't like hunting or fishing, give 'em a camera. Tell them to shoot a particular critter; say, a Blue Jay. Off they go, learning woodsman-ship without even knowing it.

GET IT INTO THE SCHOOLS

Hunting, gun safety, fishing, trapping and other conservation tools SHOULD BE TAUGHT in schools where these activities are likely to occur in the nearby woods.

I saw a TV spot recently; high-school kids have a skeet & trap team. (Nebraska) By the way, they've never had an "accident".

Mathews Archery has made a good dent, getting archery in some schools. With their new variable draw length Genesis bow, just about everyone can shoot the same bows. By minimizing costs, plenty of kids & teachers have discovered the joy of flinging arrows. This improves teacher-student relationships. The kids get to see teachers in a different light; learning retention & attendance automatically goes sky-high.

Recently we're seeing the evolution of college team fishing tournaments. These, too, are great strides. Once the outdoors are valued more, society will respect them more. The thing will snowball.

TAKE BACK THE STREETS
ELIMINATE DRUG ABUSE

It's real simple; UNTIL we eradicate street drugs, we will have people getting shot for drugs. The cost to society is staggering; there are addicts fencing stolen goods. Officers must buy costly equipment, to deal with meth-crazed perps. There are booking fees, court costs, public defense and jail fees to house the dope addicts until trial time.

Then what happens? Our jails are full, so judges go out of their way to keep dope fiends OUT of jail. They offer 'diversion'; *"Yes, your honor, I swear I'll stick to the program THIS TIME"*! Away goes the addict. Taxpayers pay the court costs, the court-mandated therapists and doctors.

Does it work? If you ask those who are employed by the system, they'll say *'SURE it works. Look at these four people* (out of a hundred) *we got off dope!'* What else would you expect them to say when their paycheck depends on their answer?

We could easily reduce court congestion and free the system to vigorously prosecute real criminals; I'm talking about the huge waste of resources to stamp out Marijuana. I don't like Pot, but I don't like Democrats either. (Still they exist and must be tolerated) But I hate black helicopters and federal agents with automatic weapons flying over my head for the entire harvest time. It's repugnant.

What do they get, for all these prohibition tactics? Not much, unless you count the irony of driving the Pot price sky-high, to the point that foreign cartels are now skulking OUR hills, polluting OUR hunting grounds and making OUR woods unsafe. We have foreigners invading American soil, establishing perimeters with automatic weapons and claymores; if that's not war, what is?

Our dollars could be better used against meth, a nasty drug with few medicinal benefits; it's just plain evil. Our cops need help. WE the People need to do whatever it takes to rid the meth scourge and the ruthless bastards that push it to our kids.

With the funds saved by easing Pot laws (and by taxing the Pot trade) we could build more prison hospitals to house drug addicts, where they might have a shot at getting clean. If they can't get off the ice, at least we could keep 'em away from our kids. If it doesn't work, at least we tried. What we're doing now doesn't work, that's for sure.

TAKE BACK THE EDUCATION OF OUR CHILDREN

"Conformity is the jailer of freedom and the enemy of growth."
John F. Kennedy
35th Pres of the USA

Our schools once taught children to think critically. Sadly, they now teach them to conform; it is the antidote to freedom. If we dislike Big Brother so much, then why do we welcome BIG MOTHER into our schools? Why are we letting the state rear our children?

In many districts, Big Mother is distributing mind-altering narcotics to one student in five, often without a full psychiatric workup... Sometimes without the parents' knowledge, after just a five minute 'diagnosis' by a nurse or a teacher without any psychiatric training.

If you doubt me,

you haven't been paying attention.

Go to Drug-free America's website

We need to turn this 'drug worship' around.

ABOLISH THE ALLOWANCE

The allowance is Welfare for minors. You might say; *"I'm paying Buffy because she's doing homework & cleaning her room"*.

Paying Buffy to be good? Sounds like bribery to me. Just think; **Who's paying YOU** to do the laundry and take out the trash?

When my daughter turned 16 she wanted a car. I was dying to buy her one, but I knew it was wrong, so I said; *"When you make the money you can buy the car."*

Kelly got a job busing tables. Months later she bought her car. One night, a boy commented; *"Wow, must be nice to have a rich daddy!"* Kelly swelled with justified indignation; *"Hey! I bought this with my OWN MONEY! You could too, if you'd get off your lazy butt and get a job!"*

Imagine how she would've cringed, had I bought the car for her. Children need to earn money, just like you and I must. The concept of delayed gratification sets a child's course for a lifetime of productivity and high self-esteem.

END GRATUITOUS PRAISE

I doubt if it's as true in the Midwest, Bible Belt or East Coast, but our West Coast teachers praise kids for routine things, such as being on time or turning in homework. This negates the purpose of praise, which is to honor extraordinary achievement.

When we praise a child for mundane things, it warps the child's value system. Reality becomes camouflaged. The world just doesn't work that way, and everybody else knows it.

Do cops praise you for driving under the speed limit? Do doctors praise you for taking your meds? We are *supposed to* follow laws and listen to doctors, just as kids should behave and do their homework.

I have plenty of heroes; those in the **armed forces, cops and firefighters, Ted Nugent,** AND the good folks in the **NRA** that fight the hard fights and **DO EXTRAORDINARY THINGS,** at great personal sacrifice and effort.

DO YOUR KIDS A
BIG FAVOR...
SAVE YOUR PRAISE
FOR HEROES.

GIVE KIDS CHORES

Chores teach responsibility. I know a four year-old whose chore is to feed the fish. He does a better job than I do. Later, he will get bigger chores, in accordance with his growth and maturation.

Participating in after-school sports is a reward, not a chore. The kid's grades must be kept up and the chores get done or else; No more sports!

Does your boss say it's OK to skip work Monday because you played too much golf on Sunday? Work comes before play. What was good for parents (as kids) is good for today's children. The good stuff never goes out of style.

Some of today's parents are under the illusion that their kid will become president or cure cancer. Or bring world peace... *whatever.* While it's natural to envision the best for our kids, it can become an obsession, making fertile soil for exploitation. The kid starts demanding more and more; today's allowance gradually morphs into tomorrow's Porsche.

Trust me; in all likelihood, your kid will turn out to be average. If he/she ends up with a college degree and a job, you did your job. And, without a doubt, your kid's success will be partly because you had the guts to assign chores, INSTEAD of letting them coast.

CULTIVATE WINNERS, NOT SLACKERS!

"The Nation that makes a great distinction between its scholars and its warriors will have its thinking done by cowards and its fighting done by fools."

(Thucydides; 460bc-395 BC; greek historian, author, father of scientific history & political realism. His text is still studied at advanced military colleges worldwide, and the Melian Dialogue is still a valid work of international relations.)

Most of our current problems stem from poor parenting and farcical teaching methods. Our kids seem to think the world will come to them if they just lay on the couch, texting peers and playing e-games. They don't see the threat that's getting ready to kick down our door and take our food, water & resources.

Teachers betray their duty to prepare children; they spew politically correct tripe, instead of telling it like it is. They promote compromise, instead of victory. They tell our kids that the world is somehow brighter or fairer than it really is. Not only is this wrong, it is patently immoral. If this were a NON-VIOLENT world, then teaching non-violence would make perfect sense. But in the real world, billions of people fight every day for food, jobs, water and turf.

"In a perfect world, you wouldn't need guns. This is not a perfect world."

Sheriff Ben Johnson, Volusia County, Florida

To teach non-violence is to prepare our children for submission. While our kids are busy dialing 911 for every minor insult, a billion other children are fighting it out. Our kids are getting softer while others get tougher. When these two vastly different cultures collide, which group will prevail?

If the state's teachers have their way, we may end up as a nation of unarmed politically correct pacific, navel-contemplating sheep working in the salt mines for those who were better skilled in martial art. We will become what we once abhorred, the inevitable result of our delusional experiment in untrammeled pacifism and unbridled complicity.

We will find ourselves needing someone to fight for us, but there won't be any Marines left, because our teachers taught us pacifism

Did we politely ask HITLER to take a time-out? Did we mail him a sternly worded letter from NATO? Did we extend an olive branch? NO. We the People loaded up our best warriors and guns, went OVER THERE and kicked his ugly ass all over Europe. Our predecessors knew when and how to fight! Tragically, these lessons aren't taught in schools any longer. (except military academies)

When did it become Politically Correct to give up and bend over ?

If two youths have a fistfight today, they may get arrested, possibly ending up with felonies.

How can this insane policy benefit society?

Does the country sleep better? Is it ethical to ruin the futures of the young men that still have the courage to fight for their principles?

At my old country school there was a fight per week; a great, natural way to bleed off excess pressure before it escalated into something more serious. The basic fist fight ain't pretty or politically correct but it balances the testosterone levels of those who partake; even the losers got respect, because they fought, instead of cowering.

Now, before you conclude that this was too violent, these fights were an effective deterrent to trash talking; something that runs rampant among youth today.

In fact, some of those fights were set up by our COACHES when they'd see the signs building up; they'd put boxing gloves on the boys and haul 'em into the wrestling room. You'd hear a few loud thumps; the door would open. Coach and both red-faced combatants would come out. They'd shake hands and that was that. The next day at practice, the combatants were friends again. It worked well. We NEVER had a schoolyard shooting.

In contrast, we now have a society in which fist fighting (or any form of touch) are routinely construed as felonious acts. Our young men can't vent that pressure; it can build to a mushroom cloud. Then, when some disturbed punks get crazy, the parenting pundits wonder why the kids went postal. It makes me wonder why school officials have adopted such ridiculous measures, which don't work, and actually cultivate extreme outcomes such as the Columbine & Sandy Hook massacres.

Meanwhile, it's as plain as the Emperor's new clothes; We're cultivating slackers, NOT winners.

Or is this whole anti-violence campaign the warning sign of a darker thing? With state revenues in the toilet, bureaucrats are looking for alternative ways to tax us. Fix-it tickets are at an all-time high. Speeding tickets will set you back a week's pay. Rowdy spouses are being booked, for merely shouting at a spouse. (verbal abuse, as a felony; can you believe it?)

In this insane society, one can almost see the perverse logic; *WHY NOT* BUST TEENAGERS? They have the most disposable dollars. The more teen-age activities that are called crimes, the more dollars pour into the system. It would explain the deliberate criminalization of heretofore legitimate pastimes. Skateboarding is now vandalism. Fist fighting is assault & battery. Placing a few phone calls to a would-be girlfriend used to be called courtship; now it's called stalking.

Given this massive erosion of social values, is it any wonder that many teachers are against guns? Consider the following quote, attributed to Deborah Prothrow-Stith (Dean, Harvard Sch Public Health).

"My view of guns is simple. I hate guns and I cannot imagine why anyone would want to own one. If I had my way, guns for sport would be registered, and all other guns would be banned."

(Well, she's right about ONE THING; she doesn't have any imagination)

Public health has morphed into just another government-paid marionette that seems more about mind control than solving public health issues.

Many spree killers were on mind-altering **prescription drugs.** And yet incredibly, on a TV show a doctor said that the kid *wasn't taking enough drugs!* Before he began treatment, Johnny would just lay on the couch. Enter the drugs; he got off the couch and shot some people. Doctors call it "motivation"... Tragically, they didn't get the dosage right before Johnny went haywire. Pity about all those funerals.

Meanwhile, Doc & host kept ranting about those damned guns. Although they DID show the kid's bedroom walls; plastered with death posters, Goth paintings scrawled with profanities, HUGE Plasma TV & entertainment center. Made me wonder if his parents ever went in his room OR if they just gave him a lot of time outs in it.

New-age parenting ploys AREN'T WORKING. WE must drop the insanity and get back to what worked. When we quit overindulging our children and start imprinting morals again, a vast array of social problems will vanish. And, we can keep our guns.

When we stop cultivating spree killers, we will stop having spree killings.

(doesn't it seem obvious?)

I'm NOT alone in this opinion. The following speech, pasted from nation.foxnews, clearly shows we've neglected our duty for decades...

"This speech was broadcast by legendary ABC Radio commentator Paul Harvey on April 3, 1965:

"If I were the Devil . . . I mean, if I were the Prince of Darkness, I would of course, want to engulf the whole earth in darkness. I would have a third of its real estate and four-fifths of its population, but I would not be happy until I had seized the ripest apple on the tree, so I should set about however necessary to take over the United States. I would begin with a campaign of whispers. With the wisdom of a serpent, I would whisper to you as I whispered to Eve: "Do as you please." "Do as you please."

To the young, I would whisper, "The Bible is a myth." I would convince them that man created God instead of the other way around. I would confide that what is bad is good, and what is good is "square". In the ears of the young marrieds, I would whisper that work is debasing, that cocktail parties are good for you.

I would caution them not to be extreme in religion, in patriotism, in moral conduct. And the old, I would teach to pray. I would teach them to say after me: "Our Father, which art in Washington"

If I were the devil, I'd educate authors in how to make lurid literature exciting so that anything else would appear dull and uninteresting. I'd threaten T.V. with dirtier movies and vice versa.

And then, if I were the devil, I'd get organized. I'd infiltrate unions and urge more loafing and less work, because idle hands usually work for me. I'd peddle narcotics to whom I could. I'd sell alcohol to ladies and gentlemen of distinction. And I'd tranquilize the rest with pills.

If I were the devil, I would encourage schools to refine young intellects but neglect to discipline emotions . . . let those run wild. I would designate an atheist to front for me before the highest courts in the land and I would get preachers to say "she's right." With flattery and promises of power, I could get the courts to rule what I construe as against God and in favor of pornography, and thus, I would evict God from the courthouse, and then from the school house, and then from the houses of Congress and then, in His own churches

I would substitute psychology for religion, and I would deify science because that way men would become smart enough to create super weapons but not wise enough to control them.

If I were Satan, I'd make the symbol of Easter an egg, and the symbol of Christmas, a bottle. If I were the devil, I would take from those who have and I would give to those who wanted, until I had killed the incentive of the ambitious. And then, my police state would force everybody back to work. Then, I could separate families, putting children in uniform, women in coal mines, and objectors in slave camps. In other words, if I were Satan, I'd just keep on doing what he's doing.

Paul Harvey, Good Day."

ELECT REAL LEADERS!

FIRE THE DUPLICITOUS, BLOODSUCKING LEECHES

It's time to take America back from the spineless, double-faced politicians and to replace them with REAL LEADERS who won't bow to corporate interests. WE NEED PEOPLE WHO WILL DO what's right for the People.

We must elect leaders who are PRO-Constitution, who won't just tout their pet right; gays want equal marriage, women want reproductive freedom; and THE MEDIA? Journalistic freedom. Lawyers seem only interested in the 4th & 5th amendments. We gun-lovers focus so hard on the Second that we forget that all ten are absolutely vital to a free nation. When any of these rights are trampled, WE THE PEOPLE are trampled. To really be patriots, we must exercise all of our rights and DEMAND that our leaders do the same.

If they won't defend our rights?
WE, THE PEOPLE,
SHOULD <u>FIRE 'EM</u>!

CH .257

ON THE *RESPONSIBLE*

BEARING OF ARMS

RESPONSIBLE:
1; liable to be called on to answer.
2; able to answer for one's conduct and obligations. Trustworthy; able to choose between right and wrong.

That's what the founding fathers had in mind, regarding the "well regulated militia" (WRM).

**Civil rights are only ours as long as we work
to preserve them.
And, to deserve them.**

I'm talking about RESPONSIBILITY

If you click on most anti-gun websites you're bound to see some of our black sheep. These fools think that just because they're entitled to own guns, they should be slobs about it. Here are the jerks that give a shotgun to a five-year-old or drink booze while firing guns, as if this were Dodge City in 1850. When the fence straddlers see this, they give every gun owner 'thumbs down'. We lose votes right there.

The first website I surfed showed an idiot, famous for trying to pass a bill to let people carry concealed guns into bars. Ironically, he was being booked for DUI. I don't know if the feed was true, but if so, it sure puts a damper on our cause.

**RESPONSIBLE PARENTS TAILOR
THE LESSON TO THE
CHILD'S LEVEL OF MATURATION**

Recently there was a case on the East Coast; a fool at a gun range handed a loaded machine pistol to a young boy. He fired it. The recoil from automatic fire spun it rearward, shooting him fatally while his father stood there, filming what he thought would be the boy's first experience with high-powered weapons. I was astonished that anybody would hand a machine gun to a child. That boy should have been shooting a BB gun.

BABY STEPS, PLEASE!

When we were kids, we started out with BB guns. Later we got rim-fires. Later I got a job. I bought my first twelve-gauge. My point is that each step in the maturation process was mile-stoned in accordance with proven responsibility.

But nowadays we're seeing young children holding high-powered rifles while sitting in ground blinds. Some are so small they can't even lift the rifle. They'll rest it on the window sill and blast a deer that comes to the bait. Meanwhile, Dad thinks he's doing something great, but he's actually going against the grain of responsible fatherhood.

We don't put toddlers in the batter's box to face a big league fastball. First comes tee ball, little league, high school, college ball and finally, if he proves worthy, he *MIGHT* make it to the Show and stare down a big-league heater. Likewise, you DON'T teach baby Sally to drive in an Indy car. In the same way, you'd take a six-year-old fishing for bluegills, not Marlin. Later, you go out for a day on the water for bass or walleye. Only when the lad has sufficient experience do you go offshore for bill-fish.

More to my immediate point, what is the non-hunter supposed to think when watching toddlers blasting deer on TV? They see hunting as an easy, elitist pursuit passed down to undeserving toddlers who barely have the strength to pull a trigger. I have spoken with fence-straddlers who were so turned off by these videos that they concluded that every hunter's a slob sitting on his butt, blasting baited yearlings, from the comfort of air conditioned tents.

Admittedly, some celebs say they learned to hunt that way and they turned out to be good, so they extrapolate to others. Yet, one must wonder whether the few wins outweigh the many invisible losses; for every person that likes such a video, many others (voters) probably hate it.

Responsibility is the key

We have the right to keep and bear arms, but that doesn't mean we ought to abuse it. We certainly DON'T NEED more fence-straddlers being repulsed by graphic kill videos, Uzi-brandishing children and bloated deer tied to luggage racks. So the next time you see some jerk making us all look bad, set him straight. It's our duty.

**"Men fight for liberty
and win it with hard knocks.
Their children, brought up easy,
let it slip away again; poor fools.
And their grand-children are
once more slaves."**
D. H. Lawrence

"Do not separate text
from historical background.
If you do, you will have perverted
and subverted the Constitution,
which can only end in a distorted,
bastardized form of illegitimate
government."
James Madison
(He must be turning over in his grave)

Currently, there's a movement by the
Muslim population to have
all mention of the Holocaust removed
from history accounts.
They say it's 'offensive' to the Nation of Islam.
They say the holocaust was a hoax.

I say that HOLOCAUST DENIAL
is offensive to the survivors
of millions of massacred people.
Wouldn't you?

Join Hunters' & Anglers' groups

Yes, I know, it's not about hunting, but... hunters & anglers channel huge funds into the political arena. Hunting keeps us focused, as a group. For many of us it's the main force driving us into our forests each year. It keeps us in touch with with our blood brothers and it keeps our spirit alive.

Look into the eyes of another angler or hunter; you see America. You see integrity. You see a person who's not afraid to get dirty, wet or uncomfortable, if it means someone else in the camp might tag a deer or land a steelhead. You're staring straight into the eyes of the **well regulated militia.**

So why not join? Speak your mind; get known as a straight arrow with a good spine. (Pun intended) While you're at it, search the animal rights' websites; see how much they spend to restore wetlands or help wild species. It would make a great laminated card to distribute. Until we confront these big-mouths they'll whine about the gun owner, the angler, hunter & trapper. We need to say...

PUT YOUR MONEY WHERE YOUR MOUTH IS!

Hunting, fishing and trapping are ETHICAL, fundamental conservation tools that preserve the biota in a constantly shrinking world. We should NEVER shrink when someone points a finger and says; *"GUN LOVER! Hunter! EVIL BARARIAN!"*

We should straighten up and say

"DAMN RIGHT I'M A HUNTER!

WHY AREN'T YOU?"

It's well-known among biologists and conservationists that HUNTING is the best way to protect the SURVIVAL of a species. Look at today's threatened species; Orangutans, Pandas, a couple of weird storks, were POACHED to near-extinction. Got that? Poaching decimates species who cannot reproduce fast enough to overcome the losses to poaching, deforestation and habitat encroachment.

In contrast, money from hunting supports scientific management, restores habitat, funds wildlife refuges and wardens to protect the resource from poaching and other forms of over-utilization such as black-market live-animal trading.

When critics claim that hunters are only doing this so we can shoot more beasts, it's partly true, but plenty of non-game species benefit from the habitat improvements that come from hunter's dollars. But what's more true is that... they're clouding the issue with emotion. We must challenge them. Ask to see THEIR list of habitat improvements. Better yet,

just ask the anti-gunners;
"HOW MANY HOMELESS
DID *YOU FEED* LAST YEAR?"

Outdoor philanthropic groups donate tons of organic meat and fish to the hungry, every year.

Let's see PETA top THAT!

KILL THE EUPHEMISMS

Except for a few situations discussed later in this chapter, we have no need for euphemisms. I get nervous whenever I hear people spewing them. Our government loves the euphemism. Politicians & spin doctors are keen on 'em, too.

The euphemism is just psychic lubricant,

to ease penetration;

you can bet that something painful

is coming, real soon.

A common euphemisms on TV hunting shows is **'HARVEST'**. The guy's trying to soften the image of killing some hapless beast, as if that would work.

DON'T DISHONOR THE BEAST

BY CALLING IT A... _ROW CROP!_

According to wikipedia, 'harvest' means:

"... the process of gathering mature crops from the fields. The harvest marks the end of the growing season, or the growing cycle for a particular crop, and social importance of this event makes it the focus of seasonal celebrations such as a harvest festival..."

A crop of soybeans can't hide from the combine. CORN can't go nocturnal and evade the farmer. TIMBER cannot escape the chainsaw.

On the OTHER HAND, can a deer hide from hunters? Can it slink away? Can it adapt & learn new survival patterns? They're quite good at it, actually. Fish & Game stats show that 90% of hunters get skunked each year. Does that sound like we're *harvesting* deer? When you wake up at three AM, slog through mud, then sit your butt down in a wet duck blind and shiver until shooting light...

**You fire twenty rounds
to bag one measly teal...
did you REALLY *HARVEST* IT?**

If a farmer combined ten acres of corn and harvested just one ear, he'd be the worst farmer on earth. To say we harvest an animal implies that hunting wild game is as easy as picking lettuce. It disrespects wild animals and their countless eons of selective adaptation to a hostile world that's chock-full of predators, inclement weather, pathogens and other biological stressors. Using euphemisms paints us as double-talking affluent slobs who are perfectly capable of taking dumb critters at our leisure. It isn't true, but that's how it looks to others.

**If you've ever hunted elk

at 8 thousand feet,

you already know;

*ELK AIN'T LETTUCE, BABY!***

You'll NEVER hear a cop say;

"I HARVESTED A RAPIST"

Still, I must admit; this euphemism usually comes from a well-intentioned person who's trying to convey the truth, that hunters only take surplus animals from a sustainable, renewable resource.

In certain managed-farm situations, perhaps harvest is the appropriate term. After all, those deer farmers constantly tend to their 'crop'. They fence their deer in, provide feed crops, sometimes they use artificial insemination, veterinary care and record-keeping, to grow super-deer.

But aside from that situation, I'm uncomfortable with the term.

Does a scientist say;
"A HAWK HARVESTS A MOUSE?"

Scientists abhor euphemisms. I challenge you to find one scientific description of any apex predator harvesting its prey. We kill our prey, just like other predators kill theirs. Lions kill gazelles. Eagles kill rabbits. Wolves kill elk. It's time to tell it the way it is, amigos; no apologies, no sugar-coating.

When we get lucky enough to tag a deer or catch a mess of catfish, it's time to grin proudly! Our dollars support sustainable yield plans crafted by expert, scientific management. What's wrong with that?

Celebrate your success... say;

"Look at this deer I shot!

I can't wait to eat it!"

At least your critics will hate you 'cuz you're a barbarian, but they can't call you a two-faced jerk that hides behind euphemisms to conceal your actions.

So tell it like it is, not how those spindly-legged, pot-bellied gun-hating couch potatoes want you to tell it!

KILL the euphemism,

Don't harvest it!

CH .264

QUOTES
WORTH
KNOWING

"A woman who demands further gun control legislation is like a chicken

who roots for Colonel Sanders."

Larry Elder (radio & talk show host)

"The true soldier fights not because he hates what is in front of him,

but because he loves what is behind him."

G. K. Chesterton (English writer, @ turn of 20th C)

"That rifle on the wall of the labourer's cottage

or working class flat is the symbol of democracy. It is our job to see that it stays there."

George Orwell

"Among other evils which being unarmed brings you, it causes you to be despised."

Charlton Heston

"The two most important rules in a gunfight: always cheat and always win."

Clint Smith

"The world is filled with violence.
Because criminals carry guns,
we decent law-abiding citizens
should also have guns.
Otherwise they will win
and decent people will lose"
James Earl Jones

"Banning gun shows to
reduce violent crime
will work about as well
as banning auto shows
to reduce drunk driving."
Bill McIntire

"Americans have the will to resist
because you have weapons.
If you don't have a gun,
freedom of speech has no power."
Yoshimi Ishikawa

"Certainly one of the chief guarantees of freedom... is the right of the citizens to keep and bear arms. This is not to say that firearms should not be carefully used and that definite safety rules of precaution should not be taught and enforced. **But the right of the citizens to bear arms is just one guarantee against arbitrary government and one more safeguard against a tyranny which now appears remote in America, but which historically has proved to be always possible."**
Hubert H. Humphrey, 1960

**"All we have of freedom
all we use or know
This our fathers bought for us
long and long ago."**
Joseph Rudyard Kipling

"... I'm used to having a few guns around to protect me." Loretta Lynn

"As a card-carrying member of the liberal media, producing this piece was an eye opening experience. I have to admit that I saw guns as inherently evil, violence begets violence, and so on. I have learned, however, that in trained hands, just the presence of a gun can be a real "man stopper." I am sorry that women have had to resort to this, but wishing it wasn't so won't make it any safer out there." **Jill Fieldstein, CBS producer, Street Stories: Women and Guns:29 April 1993.**

Here's a favorite, from Dr. Arthur Kellerman...

**"If you've got to resist,
your chances of being hurt are less,
the more lethal your weapon.
If that were my wife, would I want her to
have a .38 Special in her hand? Yeah."**
(Health Magazine, March/April 1994)

**"Today, we need a nation of Minutemen,
citizens who are not only prepared to
take arms, but citizens who regard
the preservation of freedom
as the basic purpose of their daily life
and who are willing to consciously
work and sacrifice for that freedom."**

John Fitzgerald Kennedy

RELIGIOUS LEADERS' QUOTES

"But if someone has a gun and is trying to kill you ... it would be reasonable to shoot back with your own gun."
Dalai Lama

" ... the right to defend one's home and one's person when attacked

has been guaranteed through the ages

by common law."
Martin Luther King

"When a strong man armed keepeth his palace, his goods are in peace."
Luke 11:21, 1769 Oxford KJB

"Though defensive violence will always be 'a sad necessity'

in the eyes of men of principle,

it would be still more unfortunate if wrongdoers should dominate just men."
St. Augustine

"Without doubt one is allowed to resist against the unjust aggressor to one's life, one's goods or one's physical integrity; sometimes, even 'til the aggressor's death.... In fact, this act is aimed at preserving one's life or one's goods and to make the aggressor powerless.

Thus, it is a good act,

which is the right of the victim."
Thomas Aquinas

CH .270

STAND YOUR GROUND!

The right to stand your ground is among the oldest laws of civilization and yet the anti-gunners try to shame us for defending self, loved ones or our livelihood. My heartfelt opinion is simple... If you defend yourself, you shouldn't have to spend one hour in jail. SO... All I can say is...

HIP, HIP, HOORAY FOR MONTANA!

The good folks there won't arrest you for defending yourself, until they know you did something wrong. It's time that every state did the same, to help lawful citizens protect themselves.

In my state (CA), the shooter is often arrested. This is immoral and despicable. They don't jail COPS when they shoot in self defense; cops remain free until the investigation proves it was a bad shoot.

If you've never been busted you might think; "what's the big deal?" First of all they'll confiscate your weapon. Good luck getting it back. They'll throw you in a squad car. There's the booking fee. Your mug shot on the internet, alongside drunk drivers, wife beaters and drug addicts. Good luck with having your acquaintances reading the small print "Innocent 'til proven guilty."

You'll post bond, with a lien against the home you just defended, and another five grand up front for a lawyer, even if it doesn't go to trial; you're out eleven K or more before you get to the arraignment.

Meanwhile, the thug you repelled is in the hospital, getting killer drugs, fondling hot nurses, eating good food and has two lawyers; one for the criminal trial, one to sue your ass blind in civil court. It will cost you AT LEAST fifty grand to defend the civil, even if you're found not guilty in criminal court.

Meanwhile, you're sitting in a cell, waiting to talk to your shark. A camera spies on you. The cops place a snitch in your cell to help convict you. Your boss is wondering where you are. If you're self employed you lose business as word spreads that you're a jailbird.

At the arraignment, let's say the judge had a good night's sleep and nobody pissed him off yet today. Miraculously, the judge says; "Hey wait, you were just defending yourself; you're free to go!"

Run, don't walk; try not to worry about that eleven grand. It's gone, but the truth is, nobody gets off Scott-free when they shoot somebody. Focus on the upside... *You're not guilty!"*

Forget about the civil suit, coming later. (even if the assailant's dead,the survivors can sue you.) Celebrate that you and your loved ones are ALIVE.

Sounds good, right? Too bad it RARELY plays out that way.

When the trial begins, the prosecutor will vilify you for defending yourself. Now comes the part that nobody prepared you for. They'll claim that..

You should have dialed 911,

left your house, used non-lethal force,

locked your doors & windows,

used a security system,

and tried to reason with your attacker

or you should have just surrendered.

Or whatever.

With gun-related civil trials, craziness infects the court & jury. It should be illegal for a criminal to sue for injuries incurred while committing a crime. Likewise, it should be prevailing law across the nation, that you remain free until the police find that you actually did something wrong. WE freedom-loving patriots ought to pull together to make such legislation the nation-wide standard. It is time to give law-abiding citizens AT LEAST as much power as the crooks have.

Standing your ground is our birthright,

and should NOT result in sanctions

Some people want you lose your right to defend yourself. Many of these people are already in positions of influence. Regard the Clinton statements seen earlier. Quotes like those, which disregard the value of civil rights, pave the way for despotism.

I can't forget the Tiananmen Square protest of 1989. Thousands of dissidents tried to peacefully protest for reform. Unarmed Chinese citizens don't have the right to petition for redress. The government rolled tanks into the square; they opened fire. Hundreds were killed. That is how every society that disregards civil rights settles disputes... Shoot 'em, hang 'em, OFF WITH THEIR HEADS; LET THEM EAT CAKE!

"Where rights secured by the Constitution are involved,

there can be no rule making

or legislation which would

abrogate them."

Miranda vs. Arizona, 384 US 436 p. 491

CH .30-30

FULLY AUTOMATIC TIDBITS

(copied & pasted from various websites,
credited later)

WHY I CARRY A GUN
(edited for space)

"My old grandpa said to me 'Son, there comes a time in every man's life when he stops bustin' knuckles and starts bustin' caps And usually it's when he becomes too old to take an ass whoopin.'

I don't carry a gun to kill people.
I carry a gun to keep from being killed.

I don't carry a gun to scare people.
I carry a gun because this world's be a scary place.

I don't carry a gun because I'm paranoid.
I carry a gun because there are real threats in the world..

I don't carry a gun because I'm evil.
I carry a gun because I have lived long enough to see the evil in the world.

I don't carry a gun because I hate the government.
I carry a gun because I understand the limitations of government..

I don't carry a gun because I'm angry.
I carry a gun so that I don't have to spend the rest of my life hating myself for failing to be prepared.
I don't carry a gun because I want to shoot someone.
I carry a gun because I want to die at a ripe old age in my bed, and not on a sidewalk somewhere.

I don't carry a gun because I'm a cowboy.
I carry a gun because, when I die and go to heaven,
I want to be a cowboy.

I don't carry a gun to make me feel like a man.
I carry a gun because men know how to take care of
themselves and the ones they love.

I don't carry a gun because I feel inadequate.
I carry a gun because unarmed and facing three
armed thugs, I am inadequate.

I don't carry a gun because I love it.
I carry a gun because I love life and the people who
make it meaningful to me.

Police protection is an oxymoron.
Free citizens must protect themselves.

Police do not protect you from crime, they just
investigate the crime after it happens.

Mostly, I carry a gun because I'm too young to die
and too old to take an ass whoopin"

(author unknown)

GUN CONTROL HISTORY LESSON

GUN CONTROL ACHIEVED:

RESULT:

GUN CONTROL ACHIEVED:		RESULT:
1929 Soviet Union	By 1959	20 million dissidents exterminated
1911 Turkey	By 1917	1.5 million Armenians exterminated
1938 Germany	By 1945	13 million Jews & others exterminated
1935 China	1948-52	20 million dissidents exterminated
1964 Guatemala	By 1981	100,000 Mayan Indians exterminated
1970 Uganda	By 1979	300,000 Christians exterminated
1956 Cambodia	1975-77	1 million educated people exterminated

GUN CONTROL in 20th CENTURY CAUSED 56 MILLION PEOPLE TO BE MURDERED!

WHAT WILL THE TOLL BE IN 21ST CENTURY?

TAKE A LOOK AT DARFUR, SOMALIA, THE CONGO...
It does *not look good.*

Following from buckeye . Com famous gun quotes

"I have a love interest in every one of my films - a gun." **Arnold Schwarzenegger**

"I have a very strict gun control policy: if there's a gun around, I want to be in control of it." **Clint Eastwood**

"The world is filled with violence. Because criminals carry guns, we decent law-abiding citizens should also have guns. Otherwise they will win and the decent people will lose."
James Earl Jones

"An armed society is a polite society."

&

"There are no dangerous weapons. There are only dangerous men."
Robert A. Heinlein

"We would just go out and line up a bunch of cans and shoot with rifles, handguns and at times, submachine guns... When I was a kid it was a controlled atmosphere, we weren't shooting at humans... we were shooting at cans and bottles mostly. I will most certainly take my kids out for target practice."

Johnny Depp

*"Now they're tryin' to take my guns away
And that would be just fine
If you take 'em away from the criminals first
I'd gladly give you mine"*

Charlie Daniels Band, 'A Few More Rednecks

"Foolish liberals who are trying to read the Second Amendment out of the constitution by claiming it's not an individual right or that it's too much of a safety hazard don't see the danger of the big picture. They're courting disaster by encouraging others to use this same means to eliminate portions of the Constitution they don't like."

Alan Dershowitz (admittedly an anti-gunner, WHICH makes his quote all the more compelling. He's bright enough to see what lies behind such a foolish act as unraveling a portion of the Constitution.

founding fathers gun-quotes

(The following from buckeye website)

"A free people ought not only to be armed and disciplined,

but they should have sufficient arms

and ammunition to maintain a status

of independence from any who might attempt to abuse them, which would include their own government."

George Washington

"Those who would give up

essential liberty

to purchase a little temporary safety, deserve neither liberty nor safety."

Benjamin Franklin

DAMN, we sure could have used Ben when they passed the Patriot Act! Never have Americans sacrificed so much liberty. And for what... the Homeland Security department? *RAW DEAL!!!*

What a bunch of suckers we must be, to let such a law stay on the books. WE need to repeal it, forthwith.

QUOTES ATTRIBUTED TO
THOMAS JEFFERSON

I wanted to sequester some quotes from certain founders; their intent and passion had profound impact in forming our constitution. To start it off... *here's Tommy.*

Thomas Jefferson, 4/13/1743 – 7/4/1826. American Founding Father. Principal author of the U.S. Declaration of Independence. Third president, (1801-09). Served in Continental Congress. Wartime governor of Virginia. In 1784 began diplomat, then Minister to France. 1790, 1st US Sec Of State.

It's not so well known that along w/ J. Madison he wrote secret documents to oppose a national bank. Or that he orchestrated the Louisiana Purchase and sent Lewis and Clark on their expedition.

He was a tobacconist & slave owner, and probably fathered Sally Hemings' (his slave) six children. Perhaps that didn't set him apart from his peers, but this did; he spoke five languages, delved into science, religion and philosophy. His views on slavery changed over time, much more so than others of his genre, although today's critics still criticize him for his stance.

NONETHELESS, Jefferson's views on arming the People were consistent and brilliantly simple. It's difficult to find any doubt or confusion in his words.

"The strongest reason for people to retain the right to keep and bear arms is, as a last resort, to protect themselves against tyranny in government."

&

"No free man shall ever

be debarred the use of arms."

&

"The laws that forbid the carrying of arms... disarm only those who are neither inclined nor determined to commit crimes.... Such laws make things worse for the assaulted and better for the assailants; they serve to encourage rather than to prevent homicides, for an unarmed man may be attacked with greater confidence than an armed man."

(This last quote; Thomas Jefferson quoting 18th century criminologist Cesare Beccaria)

Thomas Jefferson's quotes, cont'd

"A strong body makes the mind strong. As to the species of exercises, I advise the gun. While this gives moderate exercise to the body, it gives boldness, enterprise and independence to the mind. Games played with the ball, and others of that nature, are too violent for the body and stamp no character on the mind. Let your gun therefore be your constant companion of your walks." (TJ, writing to his teenaged nephew)

"The Constitution of most of our states (and of the United States) assert that all power is inherent in the people; that they may exercise it by themselves; **that it is their right and duty to be at all times armed."**

(Obviously, they wanted the citizenry armed and ready to fight any such breaches from any NEW GOVERNMENT. If that doesn't do it for you, keep reading!)

"On every occasion [of Constitutional interpretation] let us carry ourselves back to the time when the Constitution was adopted, recollect the spirit manifested in the debates, and instead of trying [to force] what meaning may be squeezed out of the text, or invented against it, [instead let us] conform to the probable one in which it was passed."

Quite clear, isn't it?

Thomas Jefferson's quotes, cont'd

Here's one of my all-time favorites... (Bold added, as usual)

"I enclose you a list of the killed, wounded, and captives of the enemy from the commencement of hostilities at Lexington in April, 1775, until November, 1777, since which there has been no event of any consequence ... I think that upon the whole it has been about one half the number lost by them, in some instances more, but in others less. **This difference is ascribed to our superiority in taking aim when we fire; every soldier in our army having been intimate with his gun from his infancy."**

(in a letter to Giovanni Fabbroni, 6 / 8 / 1778)

It sounds like Jefferson was bragging that our boys shot better than the British did. Further, that this was due to the fact that our boys grew up shooting guns; essentially reinforcing the "militia" as conceptualized in the Second Amendment.

In contrast, Britain's soldiers were professionals, having spent most of their lives drilling, marching, etc, but not as our militia did, hunting the woods & shooting deer, squirrels and birds on the fly.

QUOTES ATTRIBUTED TO JAMES MADISON

James Madison Jr. was born in 1751, died 1836. He was the 4th U.S. President, known as the "Father of the Constitution". Not only that, but Madison was also the dominant champion of the Bill of Rights.

Just as Jefferson, Madison was also a slave owner. He was old-money, having inherited tobacco land. So yes, Madison was a career politician, an elitist by today's standards; which makes it all the more intriguing that he championed the rights of the common man.

In 1789 he became the leader in the House of Representatives, drafting many basic laws for our new country. But his biggest role had to be that of drafting the Bill of Rights. It's fair to say that nobody had a clearer intent about its message.

But later in his presidency, Madison led us into the War of 1812, which didn't go well. He had troubles with inland Indians who were British allies. He saw the need for better administration, as well as a national bank and a stronger federal government, which were two things he had long resisted.

James Madison quotations

"Arms in the hands of citizens may be used at individual discretion in private self defense"

"Americans have the right and advantage of being armed, unlike the people of other countries, whose leaders are afraid to trust them with arms."

"The right of the people to keep and bear arms shall not be infringed. A well regulated militia, composed of the body of the people, trained to arms, is the best and most natural defense of a free country."

"The ultimate authority resides in the people alone."

"A government resting on the minority is an aristocracy, not a Republic, and could not be safe with a numerical and physical force against it, without a standing army, an enslaved press and a disarmed populace."

QUOTES ATTRIBUTED TO GEORGE MASON

George Mason lived from 1725-'92. He refused to sign the Constitution because it lacked a bill of rights. Earlier, he drafted the Virginia Declaration of Rights, so when his peers finally caved to his pressure, he based the U.S. Constitution's Bill of Rights largely upon those already drafted for Virginia. Because of that, George Mason is known as the Father of the Bill of Rights, along with James Madison.

He, too, was a slaveholder, but he wanted to ban further importation of slaves, to keep it from spreading to other states. As for where it existed, Mason wanted to preserve the status quo, fearing that to abolish slavery there would cause too much chaos and bloodshed. Besides that, he considered it to be UN-winnable.

"To disarm the people is the most effectual way to enslave them."

&

"I ask sir, what is the militia? It is the whole people except for a few politicians."

(don't ya love that one?)

QUOTES ATTRIBUTED TO PATRICK HENRY

Born in 1736, died in 1799; Henry was an orator & governor of Virginia several times. He led the opposition to the Stamp Act, he vigorously opposed corruption in government and basically championed the cause of freedom.

After the Revolution he led the anti-federalists in Virginia, who opposed the Constitution because it threatened states' rights and individual freedoms; which makes the following quotes all the more credible.

"...Give me liberty or give me Death!"

&

"Guard with jealous attention the public liberty. Suspect everyone who approaches that jewel. Unfortunately, nothing will preserve it but downright force. Whenever you give up that force, you are ruined.... The great object is that every man be armed. Everyone who is able might have a gun."

"Are we at last brought to such humiliating and debasing degradation, that we cannot be trusted with arms for our defense? Where is the difference between having our arms in possession and under our direction and having them under the management of Congress? If our defense be the real object of having those arms, in whose hands can they be trusted with more propriety, or equal safety to us, as in our own hands?"

Patrick Henry

QUOTES ATTRIBUTED TO
SAMUEL ADAMS

Sam Adams (the statesman, not the beer) lived from 1722-1803. He was a second cousin to John Adams, president.

Sam strenuously opposed excessive taxation by the Brits. He coordinated communication among the other patriots in the colonies, developed and printed circulars and basically raised hell against the British. The upshot was the Boston Tea Party, which kick-started the American Revolution.

Some critics claim that he started this too early, that he was a crap-stirring propagandist who incited violence to achieve his own personal ends. Whatever... The man is now hailed as a hero, without whom we'd still be paying the King's taxes, eating bangers and spotted dick.

How did he stand on bearing arms? Without arms, it's impossible to resist tyranny or to have free speech. Well, turn the page; see for yourself.

"The Constitution shall never be construed to prevent the people of the United States who are peaceable citizens from keeping their own arms."

Samuel Adams

This quote interests me because it mentions "peaceable citizens.' Considering what he started, it smolders of hypocrisy, eh?

Well, at least he covered it with 'keeping their own arms,' making a distinction between private ownership and governmental warehousing of firearms. (Which was later done by England in the embryo stages of total gun confiscation; the citizens had to store their guns in police precincts. And then later, the police simply refused access. Game over... Simple as that.

But I can read between the lines, too; old Sam knew that even in those early times, the 'non-peaceable' citizens would surely have weapons, regardless of legislation. So there you had the slogan for a bumper sticker, which took another 200 years to get here...

"When guns are outlawed,
only outlaws will have guns."

QUOTES ATTRIBUTED TO RICHARD HENRY LEE

Richard H. LEE, 1732-94, was one of the first president pro temps of the U.S. Senate. He called for the resolution to form the Declaration of Independence. He was also Robert E. Lee's uncle.

"To preserve liberty, it is essential that the whole body of the people always possess arms, and be taught alike, especially when young, how to use them."

&

"A militia, when properly formed, are in fact the people themselves ... and include all men capable of bearing arms."

The next time some gun-hating simpleton tries to tell you that the "militia" means armed forces OR ANYTHING OTHER THAN THE PEOPLE... shove this quote right down his (or her) throat.

There's NO doubt about it!

ATTRIBUTED TO ALEXANDER HAMILTON

Hamilton lived from 1757; possibly earlier, in 1755. Caribbean birth records might have been wrong. He was a Founding Father, economist & one of America's first constitutional lawyers. As the Secretary of the Treasury, he authored the economic policies of George Washington. (He died in 1804, from wounds from a famous pistol duel with Aaron Burr, sitting Vice President, but that's another story)

" ... for it is a truth, which the experience of all ages has attested, that the people are commonly most in danger when the means of insuring their rights are in the possession of those of whom they entertain the least suspicion."

&

"The best we can help for concerning the people at large is that they be properly armed."

(*Hamilton,* The Federalist Papers at 184-8)

PRO-GUN QUOTES ATTRIBUTED TO OTHERS

"This may be considered as the true palladium of liberty.... The right of self defense is the first law of nature: in most governments it has been the study of rulers to confine this right within the narrowest limits possible. Wherever standing armies are kept up, and the right of the people to keep and bear arms is, under any color or pretext whatsoever, prohibited, liberty, if not already annihilated, is on the brink of destruction."

St. George Tucker

"... arms ... discourage and keep the invader and plunderer in awe, and preserve order in the world as well as property.... Horrid mischief would ensue were (the law-abiding) deprived the use of them."

Thomas Paine

"The right of the citizens to keep and bear arms has justly been considered, as the palladium of the liberties of a republic; since it offers a strong moral check against the usurpation and arbitrary power of rulers; and will generally, even if these are successful in the first instance, enable the people to resist and triumph over them."

Joseph Story

"What, Sir, is the use of a militia? It is to prevent the establishment of a standing army, the bane of liberty.... Whenever Governments mean to invade the rights and liberties of the people, they always attempt to destroy the militia, in order to raise an army upon their ruins."

Rep. Elbridge Gerry of Massachusetts

"We have no government armed with power capable of contending with human passions unbridled by morality and religion. Avarice, ambition, revenge, or gallantry, would break the strongest cords of our Constitution as a whale goes through a net. **Our Constitution was made only for a moral and religious people. It is wholly inadequate to the government of any other.**"

John Adams

Adams hit the bull's eye; when society loses its morals and religion, it sows the seeds of its destruction. When guns are in the hands of moral and religious people they aren't used for criminal acts, but rather, to stop criminals.

The only thing that can stop

a bad man with a gun...

is a good man or woman

with a gun.

Clearly, the framers intended for
every able person
to be armed,

To protect self, family and property
against criminals
AND
government gone bad.

To quote Ted Nugent;

*"WHICH PART
DON'T YOU GET?"*

OTHER QUOTES

(pasted from various websites)

"In a perfect world,
you wouldn't need guns.
This is not a perfect world."
Sheriff Ben Johnson, Volusia County, Florida

"The West was not won
with a registered gun."
unknown

"The problem is not the
availability of guns,
it is the
availability of morons."
Antonio Meloni

"Know guns, no crime. No guns, know crime."
Ralph Lauretano

"A shoot-out is better than a massacre!"
David Bennett

QUOTATIONS FROM
THE ANCIENTS

**"A sword never kills anybody;
it is a tool in the killer's hand."**

Lucius Annaeus Seneca

(4bc-65ad; Roman statesman, adviser to Nero)

**"I will teach my children weapons
and warfare, so they might teach their
children science and law, so they might
teach their children art and literature."**

Unknown Greek

**"Freedom is the sure possession

of those alone who have

the courage

to defend it."**

Pericles

(495-429 bc, greek statesman, gen. Of Athens in
golden age)

"Though defensive violence
will always be 'a sad necessity'
in the eyes of men of principle,
it would be still more unfortunate
if wrongdoers should dominate just men."

St. Augustine,

(354-430 AD. Philosopher, theologian, influential in
development of Western Christianity)

"From his weapons on the open road
no man should step one pace away;
you don't know for certain
when you're out on the road
when you might
have need of your spear"

Havamal

(Viking-age collection of common sense)

Here ends the ancient quotes..

(following online quotes attributed to Clint Smith, President and Director of Thunder Ranch®, a Marine Corps veteran of two infantry and Combined Action Platoon tours in Vietnam. His experience includes seven years as a police officer during which he served as head of the Firearms Training Division as well as being a S.W.A.T. member and precision rifleman.

"I carry a gun because a cop is too heavy."

"An armed man will kill an unarmed man with monotonous regularity."

"When seconds count, the cops are just minutes away."

"A reporter did a human-interest piece on the Texas Rangers. The reporter recognized the Colt Model 1911 the Ranger was carrying and asked him...

'Why do you carry a 45?
The Ranger responded,
'Because they don't make a 46.'

"The purpose of fighting is to win. There is no possible victory in defense. The sword is more important than the shield, and skill is more important than either. The final weapon is the brain. All else is supplemental."

"You cannot save the planet. You may be able to save yourself and your family."

"You have the rest of your life to solve your problems. How long you live depends on how well you do it."

"You can say 'stop' or 'alto' or use any other word you think will work but I've found that a large bore muzzle pointed at someone's head is pretty much the universal language."

"Don't shoot fast, shoot good."

"If you carry a gun, people will call you paranoid. That's ridiculous. If I have a gun, what in the hell do I have to be paranoid for."

"If you're not shootin', you should be loadin'. If you're not loadin, you should be movin', if you're not movin', someone's gonna cut your head off and put it on a stick."

"Make your attacker advance through a wall of bullets. I may get killed with my own gun, but he's gonna have to beat me to death with it, cause it's gonna be empty."

"Don't forget, incoming fire
has the right of way."

"The two most important rules
in a gunfight:
Always cheat and always win."

"The handgun would not be my choice of
weapon if I knew I was going to a fight.
...I'd choose a rifle, a shotgun, an RPG or
an atomic bomb instead."

following quotes attributed to John Dean "Jeff" Cooper (May 10, 1920 - September 25, 2006) known as father of the Modern Technique of handgun shooting. Most firearm pros consider him one of the 20th century's leading experts on the use and history of small arms. Col. Cooper is noted for his no-nonsense quotations about guns and personal defense.

"One cannot legislate the maniacs off the street... these maniacs can only be shut down by an armed citizenry. Indeed bad things can happen in nations where the citizenry is armed, but not as bad as those which seem to be threatening our disarmed citizenry in this country at this time."

"Owning a handgun doesn't make you armed any more than owning a guitar makes you a musician."

"The first rule of gunfighting; have a gun."

"The police cannot protect the citizen at this stage of our development, and they cannot even protect themselves in many cases. It is up to the private citizen to protect himself and his family, and this is not only acceptable, but mandatory."

"The will to survive is not as important as the will to prevail... the answer to criminal aggression is retaliation."

"Already a couple of the faithful have sent in checks for a foundation memorial to the innocents who perished at the hands of the ninja at Waco... I have been criticized by referring to our federal masked men as 'ninja' ... Let us reflect upon the fact that a man who covers his face shows reason to be ashamed of what he is doing. A man who takes it upon himself to shed blood while concealing his identity is a revolting perversion of the warrior ethic. It has long been my conviction that a masked man with a gun is a target. I see no reason to change that view."

"One bleeding-heart type asked me in a recent interview if I did not agree that 'violence begets violence.' I told him that it is my earnest endeavor to see that it does. I would like very much to ensure — and in some cases I have — that any man who offers violence to his fellow citizen begets a whole lot more in return than he can enjoy."

"The purpose of the pistol is to stop a fight that somebody else has started, almost always at very short range."

"Bushido is all very well in its way, but it is no match for a 30-06."

"A free man must not be told how to think, either by the government or by social activists. He may certainly be shown the right way, but he must not accept being forced into it."

"**Hoplophobia** is a mental disturbance characterized by irrational aversion to weapons, as opposed to justified apprehension about those who may wield them."

"The media insist that crime is the major concern of the American public today. In this connection they generally push the point that a disarmed society would be a crime-free society. They will not accept the truth that if you take all the guns off the street you still will have a crime problem, whereas if you take the criminals off the street you cannot have a gun problem."

"In the larger sense, however, the personal ownership of firearms is only secondarily a matter of defense against the criminal. Note the following from Thomas Jefferson: The strongest reason for the people to keep and bear arms is, as a last resort, to protect themselves against the tyranny of government. That is why our masters in Washington are so anxious to disarm us. **They are not afraid of criminals. They are afraid of a populace which cannot be subdued by tyrants.**"

"Safety is something that happens

between your ears,

not something you hold in your hands."

Here's my favorite Cooper quote...

"The 1911 pistol remains the service pistol of choice in the eyes of those who understand the problem. Back when we audited the FBI academy in 1947, I was told that I ought not to use my pistol in their training program because it was not fair...

"Maybe the first thing one should demand of his sidearm is that it be unfair."

THE FOUNDING FATHERS,

ON ARMS

"Firearms stand next in importance to the constitution itself. They are the American people's liberty teeth and keystone under independence ... from the hour the Pilgrims landed to the present day, events, occurrences and tendencies prove that to ensure peace security and happiness, the rifle and pistol are equally indispensable ...the very atmosphere of firearms anywhere restrains evil interference — they deserve a place of honor with all that's good."

George Washington

"The supposed quietude of a good man allures the ruffian; while on the other hand arms, like laws, discourage and keep the invader and plunderer in awe, and preserve order in the world as property. The same balance would be preserved were all the world destitute of arms, for all would be alike; but since some will not, others dare not lay them aside **... Horrid mischief would ensue were the law-abiding deprived of the use of them.**"

Thomas Paine

In the following quotes, I DARE YOU to spot ANY WIGGLE ROOM for the anti-gunners' arguments!

"I ask, Sir, what is the militia? It is the whole people. To disarm the people is the best and most effectual way to enslave them."

George Mason, Co-author of the 2ND Amendment during Virginia's Convention to Ratify the Constitution, 1788

"A militia, when properly formed, are in fact the people themselves..."

Richard Henry Lee, Letters from the Federal Farmer to the Republic, Letter XVIII, May, 1788.

"The people are not to be disarmed of their weapons. They are left in full posession of them."

Zachariah Johnson,

(Elliot's Debates, vol. 3 "The Debates in the Several State Conventions on the Adoption of the Federal Constitution)

"... the people are confirmed by the next article in their right to keep and bear their private arms"

(*Philadelphia Federal Gazette,* June 18, 1789, Pg. 2, Col. 2, Article on the Bill of Rights)

"And that the said Constitution be never construed to authorize Congress to infringe the just liberty of the Press,

or the rights of Conscience; or to prevent the people of the United States, who are peaceable citizens, from keeping their own arms..."

Samuel Adams,

(Philadelphia Independent Gazetteer, August 20, 1789, "Propositions submitted to the Convention of this State")

"The greatest danger to American freedom is a government

that ignores the Constitution."

Thomas Jefferson, 3RD PRESIDENT

"There are men in all ages who mean to govern well, but they mean to govern. They promise to be good masters, but they mean to be masters. "

Noah Webster, American Lexicographer, 1758-1843

"The people never give up their liberties but under some delusion."

Edmund Burke British Statesman, 1784

"Necessity is the plea for every infringement of human freedom. It is the argument of tyrants; it is the creed of slaves."

William Pitt

"What country can preserve its liberties if their rulers are not warned from time to time that their people preserve the spirit of resistance. Let them take arms."

Thomas Jefferson to James Madison

CH .308

"Forgive your enemies, but never forget their names."
John F. Kennedy,
35th U.S. President

Kennedy was truly one of our best leaders. He had the stones to handle the Cuban Missile Crisis and the talent to critically distinguish between ally and enemy. He knew that no matter what the cost, freedom is ALWAYS worth it.

We owe it to future generations to remember the names of those who would strip away our right to keep and bear arms, under the mere illusion of peaceful streets.

The following anti-gun quotations ought to remind us that **many of our enemies are still out there, trying to rob us of our precious freedom.**

"One man with a gun can control 100 without one. ... Make mass searches and hold executions for found arms." **V.I. Lenin**

"The most foolish mistake we could possibly make would be to permit the conquered Eastern peoples to have arms. History teaches that all conquerors who have allowed their subject races to carry arms have prepared their own downfall by doing so."

Adolph Hitler, April 11 1942.

"Germans who wish to use firearms should join the SS or the SA - ordinary citizens don't need guns, as their having guns doesn't serve the State."

Heinrich Himmler

"If you wish the sympathy of the broad masses, you must tell them the crudest and most stupid things."

"This year will go down in history. For the first time, a civilized nation has full gun registration. Our streets will be safer, our police more efficient, and the world will follow our lead into the future!"

Adolph Hitler, 1933

"Banning guns addresses a fundamental right of all Americans to feel safe."

Diane Feinstein

"Our main agenda is to have all guns banned. We must use whatever means possible. It doesn't matter if you have to distort the facts or even lie. Our task of creating a socialist America can only succeed when those who would resist us have been totally disarmed."

Sara Brady (Chairman, Handgun Control Inc, to Senator Metzenbaum, The National Educator, January '94, P 3.)

"Our votes must go together with our guns. After all, any vote we shall have, shall have been the product of the gun. The gun which produces the vote should remain its security officer - its guarantor. The people's votes and the people's guns are always inseparable twins."

Robert Mugabe(President & big-wig, rose to power, commandeered private property, calling it "redistribution", resulting in Euro & U.S. sanctions)

"All political power comes from the barrel of a gun. The communist party must command all the guns, that way, no guns can ever be used to command the party." Mao Zedong, 1938

"The measures adopted to restore public order are: First of all, the elimination of the so-called subversive elements... They were elements of disorder and subversion. On the morrow of each conflict I gave the categorical order to confiscate the largest possible number of weapons of every sort and kind. This confiscation, which continues with the utmost energy, has given satisfactory results."

Benito Mussolini, 1931

"Those now possessing weapons and ammunition are at once to turn them over to the local police authority. Firearms and ammunition found in a Jew's possession will be forfeited to the government without compensation. Whoever willfully or negligently violates the provisions will be punished with imprisonment and a fine."

Nazi Law, Regulations Against Jews' Possession of Weapons, 1938

"I don't care if you want to hunt, I don't care if you think it's your right. I say 'Sorry.' it's 1999. We have had enough as a nation. You are not allowed to own a gun, and if you do own a gun I think you should go to prison."

Rosie O'Donnell (At around the time her bodyguard applied for a gun permit.)

How does Barack HUSSEIN feel about gun-control?

If you listen to the government-redacted, spoon-fed blurbs from the media whores, you won't see anything that tarnishes Obama... But if you want the truth, you must look elsewhere. The following paste clearly illustrates Obama's philosophy on guns and freedom. (bold & font changes added)

"The following is a narrative taken from a 2008 Sunday morning televised "Meet The Press." From Sunday's 07 Sept. 2008, 11:48:04 EST, Televised "Meet the Press" the then **Senator Obama was asked about his stance on the American Flag.** General Bill Ginn, USAF (ret.), asked Obama to explain WHY he doesn't follow protocol when the National Anthem is played. The General stated to Obama that according to the United States Code, Title 36, Chapter 10, Sec. 171... During rendition of the national anthem, when the flag is displayed, all present (except those in uniform) are expected to stand at attention, facing the flag, with the right hand over the heart. Or, at the very least, "Stand and Face It".

NOW GET THIS !!

'Senator' Obama replied:

"As I've said about the flag pin, I don't want to be perceived as taking sides..... There are a lot of people in the world to whom the American flag is a symbol of oppression.... The anthem itself conveys a war-like message. You know, the bombs bursting in air, and all that sort of thing."

(ARE YOU READY FOR THIS???)

Obama continued:, **"The National Anthem should be 'swapped' for something less parochial and less bellicose. I like the song 'I'd Like To Teach the World To Sing.' If that were our anthem, then I might salute it.** In my opinion, we should consider reinventing our National Anthem as well as 'redesign' our Flag to better offer our enemies hope and love.

"It's my intention, if elected, to disarm America to the level of acceptance to our Middle Eastern Brethren"

"If we, as a Nation of warring people, conduct ourselves like the nations of Islam, where peace prevails - - perhaps a state or period of mutual accord could exist between our governments ......"
"When I become President, I will seek a pact of agreement to end hostilities between those who have been at war or in a state of enmity, and a **freedom from disquieting oppressive thoughts.**
"We as a Nation, have placed upon the nations of Islam, an unfair injustice, which is WHY my wife disrespects the Flag, and she and I have attended several flag burning ceremonies in the past."
"Of course now, I have found myself about to become the President of the United States and I have put my hatred aside."
"I will use my power to bring CHANGE to this Nation, and offer the people a new path. My wife and I look forward to becoming our Country's First black Family. Indeed, CHANGE is about to overwhelm the United States of America."

WHAAAAAAAT, is that??? Yes, you read it right. I, for one, am speechless!!! Dale Lindsborg, <u>Washington Post</u>"

(here ends the pasted quote)

LET'S see if I'm getting it right:

OBAMA HATES AMERICA. He thinks patriotism is politically incorrect. He wants to trivialize the NATIONAL ANTHEM by reducing it to a Coke jingle. He wants to take away our guns, then kiss and make up with the (how did he put it?) *PEACEFUL* middle east. Hmmm...

He defends his wife for disrespecting the flag, which by extrapolation disrespects all who died for it and he wants us to follow him down this 'new path.' He also wants you to believe that he has PUT ASIDE his hatred of America. And, as every sociopath before him, he can't resist the urge to swing the conversation back to HIM... "I look forward to being our country's First Black Family."...

<u>NOTICE HE DIDN'T SAY</u> he looked forward to being president, just *"The First Black Family"*.

The anti-American S.O.B. should be impeached, not worshiped. As for his stance on the Second Amendment; does ANY citizen in the Islamic nation have the right to keep and bear arms?

There you go.

I disagree with his farcical characterization;

"the nations of Islam, where peace prevails."

let's see...

"Allah or the Sword"
&
"Death to the Infidels"

suicide bombers, I.E.D.s, terrorists, hijacked airliners...

(Sound peaceful?)

We Americans would have to set our clocks back 200 years, beat our women, force them to wear veils & have clitorectomies, take away their right to vote or have birth control.

Sounds real peaceful, Barack.

Whether we like it or not, America is the global police force. The "peaceful nations of Islam" tremble ONLY at the presence of our fighting soldiers and aircraft carriers.

I make no apologies for that. Neither should our "leader".

following from abcnews . go.com, 8/24/06

(edited for space, bold added)

"There are some... nearly synonymous with tyranny: **Kim Jong II, Saddam Hussein, Slobodan Milosovic...** *Yet there are other leaders... just as oppressive... ABCNEWS.com, in partnership with Human Rights Watch, has composed a list of five of the world's least known, most oppressive heads of state...*

Equatorial Guinea...Obiang Nguema... came to power... by killing his own father... he became known as the country's "torturer-in-chief." Equatorial Guinea... has a lot of oil. Its per capita income puts it near Greece and Portugal in terms of wealth, yet most people live on a dollar a day. Nguema's government... is stealing most of the money.

Turkmenistan... Saparmurat Niyazov, perhaps the most eccentric leader on the list... The education system... is dedicated... to advocating Niyazov's writing and ideology... They are forced to read his "Book of Soul"... Niyazov renamed the months of the year after his relatives and banned opera and ballet... he has also committed... atrocities... such as... to close down hospitals...

Uzbekistan — Islam Karimov... mowed down several hundred unarmed protestors... in the city of Andajan... massacre that... received little international attention. Since then Karimov... has launched a massive crackdown against dissenters... showcasing confessions that appear ... forced, just to remind people who's in charge.

Zimbabwe — Robert Mugabe... stole an election... brought a... prosperous country to its knees... using food as a weapon -- sending food aid to people who are loyal to him and denying it to people who are not. Zimbabwe under Mugabe... the closest thing...to a country being destroyed by one man."

"In compiling this list, ABC News interviewed Tom Malinowski... of Human Rights Watch. His organization monitors human rights violations... Here is a transcript of part of our discussion:

"Malinowski: ...These are people who are addicted to power and they have no moral compunction with using ruthless means for power.

"You've been in the room with oppressive leaders before, is the feeling you get sitting next to these people that much different than the people you're sitting next to right now -- do they bother you?

Malinowski: Yes... I think most Americans would... feel uncomfortable sitting in a room with someone who has killed his own people with his bare hands....

What's it like to live under a repressive regime?

Malinowski: if... **you're dealing with military people coming to your village, burning your homes and raping your women** ... the common thread is that you are treated arbitrarily by people in positions on authority -- **you can be harassed, discriminated against, you can be tortured, you can be killed often for no reason and there's nothing you can do about it.**"

(following pasted from actionforourplanet)

1.   **Zimbabwe's ruler,** President Robert **Mugabe**, has been in power since 1980... after rising to prominence in the movement against white-minority rule. Mugabe's land reform program, which involves the typically violent land seizure of farmland from white Zimbabweans attracts much criticism from foreign governments including the US and UK. The land seizure program coupled with rising inflation and poverty have caused economic meltdown in the country where the annual GDP is just $0.1 USD. **Zimbabwean police are renowned for oppressing any political dissent and torture is widespread. Every election since Mugabe came to power has been fraught with accusations of ballot box rigging.**

2... **Omar Al-Bashir has ruled Sudan with an iron fist, crushing any political dissent.** In 2009, the International Criminal Court (ICC) issued an arrest warrant for the Sudanese leader for **crimes against humanity committed in the Darfur... Since 2003, 2.7 million people have been driven from their homes as a result of Bashir's military campaigns which involve pillaging, murder, rape and torture.**

3. ... North Korea's **Kim Jong-il** repeatedly raises concerns in both South Korea and Japan... Despite North Korea's official title being The **Democratic People's Republic of Korea (DPRK), the country is anything but democratic with no elections held and all political opposition banned. Hundreds of thousands...** citizens are... **imprisoned in labour camps...** for committing petty crimes. With hoards of personal wealth, Kim Jong-il lives a lavish lifestyle whilst many of the countries people live malnourished and in poverty.

4. Burma's Senior General **Than Shwe** ruled the poverty stricken country from 1992 but officially gave up his duties as Commander-in-Chief of the Armed Forces in 2011. Shwe still holds considerable power... **to this day, free press are strictly prohibited, political gatherings are illegal...** In 2008, thousands of **protesters were massacred with many more captured, tortured and imprisoned never to be seen again.**

5. Saudi Arabia's **King Adbullah bin Abdul-Aziz Al Saud** has ruled over one of the world's most oppressive countries since 2005. **Torture, public executions, floggings and stoning without legal proceedings are all forms of capital punishment endorsed by King Abdullah and the Saudi regime**. Women... have to obtain permission from a male guardian if they want to travel, work, study or marry. Saudi women are also banned from driving and freedom of speech, opposition parties and political gatherings are also banned.

6... China's President **Hu Jintao...** promised to improve China's human rights... However, reforms never came and the countries media became even more restricted whilst religious freedoms also became more tightly controlled. **Oppression of Tibetans and ethnic groups, torture, unlawful imprisonment and a lack of labour rights...** are the subject of much criticism from human rights organisations including Amnesty International.

7... (Sayyid Ali Khameni) was president of Iran between 1981 to 1989... over 1000 intellectuals were arrested in 2010 whilst riot police used **live ammunition against anti-government protesters in 2009, following the countries rigged... election...** journalists have been imprisoned... for criticizing Khamenei's... policies.

8... Eritrea's President **Isaias Afewerki** became leader of the country in 1993... In 2008... **elections would be postponed for three or four decades...bans all human rights groups and closed down all international development agencies in 1997 in an effort to**

suppress any opposition. In 2001, 11 top government officials were arrested for petitioning the president for democratic reform. While the officials still languish in prison, they are yet to stand trial and can face execution for committing 'suspected treason'.

9... Turkmenistan's **Gurbanguly Berdymukhammedov...** presidential election, widely believed to have been rigged, with 89% of the vote. Since taking power in 2006... has failed to implement political reform or improve human rights records. Ethnic minorities such as the Baloch community are treated as subordinate second-class citizens.

10... **Muammar Al-Gaddafi...** Accused of... **torture, civilian massacres, burying people alive, and bombing civilian areas...** faces strong criticism... worldwide... has amassed a huge personal fortune of tens of billions of dollars. According to the Freedom of the Press Index, Libya is the most censored country in the Middle East and North Africa."

(paste from action ends here)

GUN CONTROL ADVOCATES...

Isaias Afewerki
King Adbullah bin Abdul-Aziz Al Saud
Muammar Al-Gaddafi
Sayyid Ali Khameni
Omar Al-Bashir
Gurbanguly Berdymukhammedov
Joseph Biden U.S. VP
Diane Feinstein SENATOR
Barack Hussein (Obama)
Adolf Hitler
Saddam Hussein
Hu Jintao
Vladimir Lenin
Robert Mugabe
Benito Mussolini
Than Shwe
Josef Stalin

To quote Barack Hussein;
It's time for a CHANGE!

BUT THAT'S ENOUGH

SPACE WASTED ON
A FEW ANTI-GUNNERS,

DON'T YOU THINK?

CH .30-06

ADDITIONAL

PRO-GUN

COMMENTS

"The only times an Afro-American
who was assaulted got away has been
when he had a gun and used it in self-defense."
Ida Bell Wells, 1862-1931
African American journalist & civil rights leader

"There is a lot of talk now about metal detectors and gun control. Both are good things. But they are no more a solution than forks and spoons are a solution to world hunger." **Anna Quindle**

"Whatever is begun in anger

ends in shame."

Benjamin Franklin

"No kingdom can be secured otherwise than by arming the people. The possession of arms is the distinction between a freeman and a slave."

"Political Disquisitions",

a British republican tract of 1774-1775

"The end move in politics is always to pick up a gun"

R. Buckminster Fuller, 1895-1983,

architect, inventor (geodesic domes)

(Following pasted from sightm1911 dot com)

"Among the many misdeeds of the British rule in India, **history will look upon the Act depriving a whole nation of arms as the blackest.** If we want the Arms Act to be repealed, if we want to learn the use of arms, here is a golden opportunity. If the middle classes render voluntary help to Government in the hour of its trial, distrust will disappear, and the ban on possessing arms will be withdrawn."
Mohandas K. Gandhi,
The Story of My Experiments with Truth, P. 403,
(Dover, 1983)

"Men trained in arms from their infancy, and animated by the love of liberty, will afford neither a cheap or easy conquest."

Declaration of the Continental Congress, 1775

"When only cops have guns, it's called a "police state".
Claire Wolfe,
"101 Things To Do Until The Revolution"

"You cannot invade mainland United States. There would be a rifle behind each blade of grass."

Admiral Yamamoto, advising Japan's leaders of the futility of invading mainland United States. It has been theorized that this was a factor in Japan's decision not to land on North America early in the war. This delay gave our industrial infrastructure time to gear up for the conflict and was decisive in our later victory.

Hmmm....

A RIFLE BEHIND EACH BLADE OF GRASS...

If that's not the CORE of a Well Regulated Militia, WHAT IS???

following from catb. Org website, (2 10 12)
(bold added for emphasis)

"The best we can hope for

concerning the people at large

is that they be properly armed."

Alexander Hamilton, Federalist Papers at 184-188

"The people of the various provinces are strictly forbidden to have in their possession any swords, short swords, bows, spears, firearms, or other types of arms. The possession of unnecessary implements makes difficult the collection of taxes and dues and tends to foment uprisings."

Toyotomi Hideyoshi, dictator of Japan, 1588

"One of the ordinary modes, by which tyrants accomplish their purposes without resistance is, by disarming the people, and making it an offense to keep arms."

Supreme Court Justice Joseph Story, 1840

"The bearing of arms is the essential medium through which the individual asserts both his

social power and his participation in politics as a responsible moral being..."

J.G.A. Pocock, describing the founders' beliefs

"Taking my gun away
because I might shoot someone
is like cutting my tongue out because I might yell
`Fire!' in a crowded theater."

Peter Venetoklis

"...quemadmodum gladius neminem occidit, occidentis telum est."

[...a sword never kills anybody; it's a tool in the killer's hand.]

Lucius A. Seneca "the Younger' @ 4 BC-65 AD

"...Virtually never are murderers the ordinary, law-abiding people against whom gun bans are aimed. Almost without exception, murderers are extreme aberrants with lifelong histories of crime, substance abuse, psychopathology, mental retardation and/or irrational violence against those around them, as well as other hazardous behavior, e.g., automobile and gun accidents."

Don B. Kates, on statistical patterns in gun crime

"The right of the citizens to keep and bear arms has justly been considered as the palladium of the liberties of a republic; since it offers a strong moral check against usurpation and arbitrary power of rulers; and will generally, even if these are successful in the first instance, enable the people to resist and triumph over them."

Supreme Court Justice Joseph Story

"Militias, when properly formed, are in fact the people themselves and include all men capable of bearing arms. **To preserve liberty it is essential that the whole body of the people always possess arms and be taught alike, especially when young, how to use them.**

Richard Henry Lee, 1788, on the 2nd Amendment

"Both oligarch and tyrant mistrust the people, and therefore deprive them of arms." **Aristotle**

(I ADMIT, I had to look up 'oligarch', but it's interesting to note that even in Aristotle's time, the few wanted the many to be disarmed.)

Oligarchy; from Greek, *(olígos)*, meaning "few", and *(archo)*, meaning "to rule or to command")... is a form of power structure, in which power effectively rests with a small number of people distinguished by royalty, wealth, family ties, education, corporate, or military control.

"Such are a well regulated militia, composed of the freeholders, citizen and husbandman, who take up arms to preserve their property, as individuals, and their rights as freemen."

M.T. Cicero, in a newspaper letter of 1788 touching the "militia" referred to in the Second Amendment to the Constitution.

"That the said Constitution shall never be construed to authorize Congress to infringe the just liberty of the press or the rights of conscience; or to prevent the people of the United states who are peaceable citizens from keeping their own arms...

Samuel Adams, in "Phila. Independent Gazetteer", August 20, 1789

"An armed society is a polite society. Manners are good when one may have to back up his acts with his life."

Robert A. Heinlein,

"Beyond This Horizon", 1942

"The right to buy weapons is the right to be free."

A.E. Van Vogt,

"The Weapon Shops Of Isher", ASF December 1942

"The danger... from armed citizens, is only to the *government*, not to *society*; and as long as they have nothing to revenge in the government (which they cannot have while it is in their own hands) there are many advantages in their being accustomed to the use of arms, and no possible disadvantage."

&

"The disarming of citizens] has a double effect, it palsies the hand and brutalizes the mind: a habitual disuse of physical forces totally destroys the moral [force]; and men lose at once the power of protecting themselves, and of discerning the cause of their oppression."

BOTH BY Joel Barlow,

"Advice to the Privileged Orders", 1792-93

"Rifles, muskets, long-bows and hand-grenades are inherently democratic weapons. A complex weapon makes the strong stronger, while a simple weapon -- so long as there is no answer to it -- gives claws to the weak."

George Orwell,

"You and the Atom Bomb", 1945

"Let us hope our weapons are never needed --but do not forget what the common people knew when they demanded the Bill of Rights: An armed citizenry is the first defense, the best defense, and the final defense against tyranny. If guns are outlawed, only the government will have guns. Only the police, the secret police, the military, the hired servants of our rulers. Only the government -- and a few outlaws. I intend to be among the outlaws."

Edward Abbey,

"Abbey's Road", 1979

"If I were to select a jack-booted group of fascists who are perhaps as large a danger to American society as I could pick today, I would pick BATF"

U.S. Representative John Dingell, 1980

"... a government and its agents are under no general duty to provide public services, such as police protection, to any particular individual citizen..."

Warren v. District of Columbia, 444 A.2d 1 (D.C. App.181)

"The conclusion is thus inescapable that the history, concept, and wording of the second amendment to the Constitution of the United States, as well as its interpretation by every major commentator and court in the first half-century after its ratification, indicates that **what is protected is an individual right of a private citizen to own and carry firearms in a peaceful manner.**"

Report of the Subcommittee On The Constitution (to) the Committee On The Judiciary, United States Senate, 97th Congress, second session (February, 1982), SuDoc# Y4.J 89/2: Ar 5/5

"In recent years it has been suggested that the Second Amendment protects the "collective" right of states to maintain militias, while it does not protect the right of "the people" to keep and bear arms. If anyone entertained this notion in the period during which the Constitution and the Bill of Rights were debated and ratified, it remains one of the most closely guarded secrets of the eighteenth century, for no known writing surviving from the period between 1787 and 1791 states such a thesis."

Stephen Halbrook,
"That Every Man Be Armed", 1984

(IF anyone claims that the 2nd is about the collective, challenge them to produce ANY writings from that era which bolster their argument.) In other words; put up or SHUT UP.

"To make inexpensive guns impossible to get is to say that you're putting a money test on getting a gun.

It's racism in its worst form."

Roy Innis,

pres. Congress of Racial Equality (CORE), 1988

"I don't like the idea that the police... seems bent on keeping a pool of unarmed victims available for the predations of the criminal class."

David Mohler, 1989, on being denied an NYC permit

*"You know why there's a
Second Amendment?
In case the government
fails to follow the first one."*

Rush Limbaugh, 17 Aug 1993

"Whether the authorities be invaders or merely local tyrants, the effect of such [gun control] laws is to place the individual at the mercy of the state, unable to resist."

Robert Anson Heinlein, 1949

"According to the National Crime Survey administered...and... the National Institute of Justice... only 12 percent of those who use a gun to resist assault are injured, as are 17 percent of those who use a gun to resist robbery. These percentages are 27 and 25 percent, respectively, if they passively comply with the felon's demands. Three times as many were injured if they used other means of resistance."

G. Kleck, "Policy Lessons from Recent Gun Control Research," Law and Contemporary Problems 49, no. 1. (Winter 1986.): 35-62.

"**If gun laws in fact worked,** the **sponsors** ... **should have no difficulty** drawing upon long lists... of criminal acts reduced by such legislation. That they cannot do so after a century and a half of trying -- that they must sweep under the rug the southern attempts at gun control in the 1870-1910 period, the northeastern attempts in the 1920-1939 period, the attempts at both Federal and State levels in 1965-1976-- establishes the repeated, complete and inevitable failure of gun laws to control serious crime."

Senator Orrin Hatch, in a 1982 Senate Report

"**Before a standing army can rule, the people must be disarmed, as they are in almost every kingdom in Europe. The supreme power in America cannot enforce unjust laws by the sword, because the people are armed, and constitute a force superior to any band of regular troops.**"

Noah Webster

"[President Clinton] boasts about 186,000 people denied firearms under the Brady Law rules. The Brady Law has been in force for three years. In that time, they have prosecuted seven people and put three of them in prison. You know, the President has entertained more felons than that at fundraising coffees in the White House, for Pete's sake."

Charlton Heston,

FOX News Sunday, 18 May 1997

"The right of self-defense is the first law of nature: in most governments it has been the study of rulers to confine this right within the narrowest limits possible... and when the right of the people to keep and bear arms is, under any color or pretext whatsoever, prohibited, liberty, if not already annihilated, is on the brink of destruction."

(Henry St. George Tucker,

in Blackstone's Commentaries)

"The biggest hypocrites on gun control are those who live in upscale developments with armed security guards -- and who want to keep other people from having guns to defend themselves. But what about lower-income people living in high-crime, inner city neighborhoods? Should such people be kept unarmed and helpless, so that limousine liberals can 'make a statement' by adding to the thousands of gun laws already on the books?"

Thomas Sowell

"Boys who own legal firearms have much lower rates of delinquency and drug use and are even slightly less delinquent than nonowners of guns."

U.S. Department of Justice, National Institute of Justice, Office of Juvenile Justice and Delinquency Prevention, NCJ-143454, "Urban Delinquency and Substance Abuse," August 1995.

"Gun Control: The theory that a woman found dead in an alley, raped and strangled...

is somehow morally superior

to a woman explaining to police

how her attacker got

that fatal bullet wound"

L.   Neil Smith

"During waves of terror attacks, Israel's national police chief will call on all concealed-handgun permit holders to make sure they carry firearms at all times, and **Israelis have many examples where concealed permit holders have saved lives.**"

John R. Lott

"Historical examination of the right to bear arms, from English antecedents to the drafting of the Second Amendment, bears proof that **the right to bear arms has consistently been, and should still be, construed as**

an individual right."

U.S. District Judge Sam Cummings,

in re U.S. vs Emerson (1999)

"Gun control" is a job-safety program for criminals.

(previous six pages pasted from catb. Org website)

"Gun control? Its the best thing you can do for crooks and gangsters. I want you to have nothing. I'm a bad guy; I'm always gonna have a gun. Safety locks? You will pull the trigger with a lock on, and I'll pull the trigger. We'll see who wins."

Sammy The Bull Gravano,

whose testimony convicted John Gotti.

"Gun control has not worked in D.C. The only people who have guns are criminals. We have the strictest gun laws in the nation and one of the highest murder rates. **It's quicker to pull your Smith and Wesson than to dial 911 if you're being robbed."**

Lieutenant Lowell Duckett,

President Black Police Caucus,

Special Assistant to Washington, D.C. Police Chief

"I am convinced that we can do to guns what we've done to drugs: create a multi-billion dollar underground market over which we have absolutely no control."

George L. Roman

"They have gun control in Cuba. They have universal health care in Cuba. So why do they want to come here?"

Paul Harvey, radio commentator, 1994

"Gun registration is a gateway drug."

Mark Gilmore

"Suppose the Second amendment said A well-educated electorate being necessary for self-governance in a free state, the right of the people to keep and read books shall not be infringed. Is there anyone who would suggest that means only registered voters have a right to read?"

Robert Levy,

Georgetown University Professor

"We should not blame a gun itself for any crime... any more than we can blame a pen for misspelling a word."

Senator Bennett (R-UT),

Congr'l Record, 5/16/68

"It is the duty of the patriot to protect his country from its government."

Thomas Paine (1737-1809),

American Revolutionary, founding father, author

"When governments fear the people, there is liberty. When the people fear the government, there is tyranny. The strongest reason for the people to retain the right to keep and bear arms is, as a last resort, to protect themselves against tyranny in government."

Thomas Jefferson (1743-1826),

founding father, 3rd US President

"Gun bans don't disarm criminals, gun bans attract them."

Walter Mondale,

Ambassador to Japan 4/20/94

"The usual road to slavery is that first they take away your guns, then they take away your property, then last of all they tell you to shut up and say you are enjoying it."

James A. Donald

"Twenty-five States allow anyone to buy a gun, strap it on, and walk down the street with no permit of any kind: some say it's crazy. However, 4 out of 5 US murders are committed in the other half of the country: so who is crazy?" Andrew Ford

"Liberalizing concealed carry laws won't lead to a return to the Wild West. ... in 19th Century cattle towns, homicide was confined to transient males who shot each other in saloon disturbances. The per capital robbery rate was 7% of modern New York City's. The burglary rate was 1%. Rape was unknown."
David Kopel - quoted in the WSJ 28 Feb 1994

China has gun control.
Afghanistan doesn't.

Seen on a bumper sticker

"After a shooting spree, they always want to take the guns away from the people who didn't do it. I sure as hell wouldn't want to live in a society where the only people allowed guns are the police and the military."

William Burroughs

"Prohibiting law-abiding people from owning guns because they might be stolen by criminals is like prohibiting women from going out at night because they might be raped."
Unknown

"A government that intended to protect the liberty of the people would not disarm them. A government planning the opposite most certainly and logically would disarm them. And so it has been in this century. Check out the history of Germany, the Soviet Union, Cuba, China and Cambodia."

Charlie Reese, syndicated columnist

"Firearms have been around for over 400 years, yet it is only in the last 20 years that people have begun shouting "gun control". Why then, only recently, has this become such an issue? Moreover, why are there more mass-murderers than at any other time in our known history?

It is not because weapons are more powerful -- 200-year-old muzzleloaders have a much greater force-per-round than today's "assault rifles". It is not because weapons are semi- or fully-automatic -- rapid-fire weapons have been available for most of the last century. It is not due to a lack of laws -- we have more "gun control" laws than ever.

It IS, however, because we have chosen to focus on "gun control" instead of crime control or "thug control." It IS because only recently has the public become complacent enough to accept, by inaction, the violence present in our society.' -

Kevin Langston, 1991

"I sympathize with people who want to ban guns, but I can't agree with them. We have to be careful in our zeal to abolish guns that we don't wind up with counter-productive legislation that will leave armed only the people most likely to do harm with them."

Hugh Downs, veteran ABC newsman

"The ruling class doesn't care about public safety. Having made it very difficult for States and localities to police themselves, having left ordinary citizens with no choice but to protect themselves as best they can, they now try to take our guns away. In fact they blame us and our guns for crime. **This is so wrong that it cannot be an honest mistake.**"

Malcolm Wallop, 1933-2011,

U.S. Sen. (R-WY)

"It is a little known (and never mentioned by the left) fact that attempts by the KKK and others in the south after the civil war to disarm newly freed blacks was a primary motivation in the passage of the Fourteenth amendment, which forbids states from abridging rights guaranteed in the Constitution and demands "equal protection of the laws".....

(Above quotes seen on freerepublic dot com)

"It is reported that in some parts of this State (South Carolina), armed parties are, without proper authority, engaged in seizing all fire-arms found in the hands of the freedmen. Such conduct is in clear and direct violation of their personal rights as guaranteed by the Constitution of the United States, which declares that "the right of the people to keep and bear arms shall not be infringed"

Union General Rufus Saxton,
reporting to the U.S.Congress circa 1870+/-, as reported in Richard Poe's *The Seven Myths of Gun Control.*

"An armed man is a citizen.
A disarmed man is a subject."

Seen on a bumper sticker

And who could forget this one?
"YOU CAN HAVE MY GUNS
WHEN YOU PRY THEM FROM MY COLD DEAD HANDS."

Charlton Heston; actor,
pro-freedom activist & patriot.

CH .44

"To my mind it is wholly irresponsible to go into the world incapable of preventing violence, injury, crime, and death.

How feeble is the mindset, to accept defenselessness.

How unnatural. How cheap.

How cowardly. How pathetic."

Ted Nugent

rock 'n roll icon, patriot, gun-owner,

my hero

A FEW GOOD SITES

I surfed the following, in preparing this book.

JUSTFACTS

Has graphic relationship between tighter gun & increased crime. (including Britain's outright ban in 1997). Other graphs show relationship b/t right to carry and reduction in crime, state by state. Check it out. I couldn't resist the urge to paste some clips.

"A 1997 survey... 18,000... inmates found that... **"30% of State offenders and 35% of Federal offenders carried a firearm when committing**"

* A 1993 ...survey of 4,977 households... at least 0.5%... had used a gun for defense during a situation in which ..."almost certainly would have been killed"... this amounts to 162,000 ... per year.

* Based on survey data from a 2000 study published in the *Journal of Quantitative Criminology*, U.S. civilians use guns to defend themselves and others... 989,883 times per year.

A 1982 survey of male felons... found...34% had been "scared off, shot at, wounded, or captured by an armed victim" 40% had decided not to commit a crime because they "knew or believed that the victim was carrying a gun"

In 1976, the Washington, D.C. City Council passed a law generally prohibiting... handguns... **During the years... in effect, the Washington, D.C. murder rate averaged 73% higher**, while the U.S. murder rate averaged 11% lower. On June 26, 2008, U.S. Supreme Court... struck down this law as unconstitutional.[35]

As you can see, suppression of personal defense firearms, even in the Nation's capital, resulted in HIGHER violent crime rates; quite the opposite of what the anti-gunners claim. Perhaps most compelling of all is the conclusion of a British study:

"...the British homicide rate has averaged 52% higher since the... 1968 gun control law and 15% higher since the... 1997 handgun ban."

You can see how helpful it is to have such statistics at hand. GO to justfacts and

GIT URSELF SOME...

MENTAL AMMO!

JPFO . ORG

well organized, coherent website.

"Three primary goals drive the ...(JPFO):

Destroy so-called "gun control" (code words for disarming innocent people).
Expose the misguided notions that lead people to seek out so-called "gun control".
Encourage Americans to understand and defend all of the Bill of Rights for all citizens. The Second Amendment is the "Guardian" of the Bill of Rights.

"Gun control" survives as an idea because most
Americans believe one single myth:
"You don't need a gun because the
police protect you from crime."

"...-- *in fact the police usually have no legal duty to protect anyone.*"

Dial 911 and Die proves this fact. For nearly every American state and territory, this book shows... **The police in most places do not even have to come when you call.**

Erase the myth of police protection, and "gun control" *dies* as an idea ... *permanently.*

"... Police help was too little, too late.
Those murderous events do not prove the need for "gun control" -- they prove the utter inability of the police to protect individuals from violent crime..."

(Also check out Richard Poe's *The Seven Myths of Gun Control... linked from jfpo site.*)

SECOND-AMENDMENT . ORG

Mostly blogs and forums, helpful with questions on the law.

CAFEPRESS

Great gun-related slogans printed on clothing, cups & bumper stickers. My favorite's a Pic of a 1911;

"The ultimate in Feminine Protection; .22 for light days, .44 for heavy days."

WFU.EDU/~ZULICK

Wake Forest's site is awesome for reference work on the constitution, preamble, etc. Highly technical, accurate and authoritative. What would you expect from a college history doc?

SIGHTM1911

Really good site, lots of quotes.

TED NUGENT . COM

A must-bookmark for EVERY freedom-lover, gun nut and hunter. It's controversial, passionate and well organized; a bit commercialized, sure... but without sponsors where would we be? Nuge's site holds many other perks, too. But what I love about Ted's massive body of work is his absolute passion and his relentless sacrifice for our liberty.

NRA.COM

**MERE WORDS DON'T
DO IT JUSTICE.
INCREDIBLE SITE;
BOOKMARK IT,
JOIN,
BE PART OF THE
SOLUTION!**

COMEANDTAKEIT

Good list of pro-gun websites, but you should click on Battle Flag's home page. Here's a paste, to wet your whistle.

Constitution Society; Organized, factual, to the point. If you want to see how the laws work in this country and in others, this site's for you.

GunOwners of America; serious as a heart attack, when it comes to pro-second data. Plenty of hot button links to sites you'll love!

Jeff Chan's Firearm Page; excellent pro-gun info

Constitution party; uncompromising, principled

NoGreaterJoy . net; good for raising children.

God and Gun Control-- good site.

GunCite . com; everything legal on gun rights, research, articles, founding fathers etc. great nav links, factual, easy to read yet deep in technical aspects. Definitely worth your time.

Students for the Second Amendment- hands-on training in Second Amendment and firearms!

CH.

.410

Sometimes you just GOTTA LAFF...

It's important to retain our sense of humor. I hope you enjoy the following jokes & tidbits, which are rich in gun-related character.

HUMOROUS QUOTES

Don't run from a sniper;
you'll just die tired.
Anon

"Guns kill people, like spoons
made Rosie O'Donnell fat."
(online quote, multiple sites)

"I carry a small pistol
to compensate for my huge penis"
(anon, internet)

"Guns don't kill people...
(Husbands that come home early
kill people)"
(anon)

"Charlie was after an outlaw and caught up with him in the vega of the river, in Val Verde County just south of the area where I used to serve as sheriff. In a flurry of action, the Ranger and the outlaw wounded each other. As he lay in the brush, Miller called over to his assailant and told him that he knew they were both wounded. Miller suggested that they stand up and finish this fight like men so that one of them could get to a doctor. In later years Miller would just shake his head and state, "And you know what? That damned fool actually stood up!"

(from the highroad . org Charlie Miller, Texas Ranger

shootingtimes. com)

"If I didn't have this gun, the King of England could walk right in here and start pushing you around. *You want that?"*
Homer Simpson

When his daughter, Gloria, informed Archie that over 85% of all murders were committed with handguns his response was, ***"Would you feel better if they were pushed outta windows?"***
All in the Family; old TV sitcom

**"Sergeant, what did you feel when
you shot that insurgent?"
Sniper; "Mostly recoil."
(anon)**

(on the fine art of negotiating a purchase)

"Did you just buy that beautiful firearm,
or are you trying
to sell that piece of crap?"

"I knew one thing: as soon as anyone
said you didn't need a gun, you'd better take
one along that worked."
Raymond Chandler

**"I love New York City; I've got a gun."
Charles Barkley**

Every humor section
SHOULD HAVE one BLOND JOKE...

A blond thinks her husband is cheating on her, so she follows him. Upon finding him in the arms of another woman, she draws her gun and puts it to her own head.
The husband yells,"No honey don't do it."

The blond yells; " Shut up! *You're next!*"

**"You can get much farther with
a kind word and a gun
than you can with
a kind word alone."**
Al Capone

**"VEGETARIANS descended from...
the WORST HUNTERS!"**
anon

"The President's hiring a new secretary; he's down to three equally qualified women. He decides to test their loyalty. Hands first woman a gun; "Your husband's in the next room. If you really love your country, go in there and shoot him."

She drops the gun; *"Oh, my hubby's GREAT! I couldn't do that!"*

Wife #2 takes the gun, fantasizes a minute, slowly gives gun back; *"I'm sorry; he's not so bad. I don't think I could... do it."*

Wife #3 grabs the gun, goes in, slams the door; six shots ring out. Man-screams happen for five minutes, then silence. She comes out, clothes ruffled, blood spattered; *"Sorry it took so long, but some idiot loaded the gun with blanks, so I had to pistol-whip him to death."*

On a sign seen in front of a house...

**"Attention thieves
My neighbor hates guns.
I respect his opinion, so
I WON'T SHOOT YOU WHEN
YOU BURGLE *HIS HOME."***

next two from military quotes dot com

"At a prewar diplomatic conference, Nazi Foreign Minister Ribbentrop "sniffed" to Eden and Churchill that if there was another war, the Italians would be on Germany's side! Churchill supposedly replied:
"That's only fair; *we had 'em last time!*"

"The reason the American Army does so well in wartime, is that war is chaos, and the American Army practices it on a daily basis."
(post-war debriefing of a German General)

"The best armor is staying out of gun-shot"
Italian proverb

"Cop, upon pulling Granny over; *"May I see your license & proof of insurance?"*
Grams shows wallet, including CCW permit.
Cop; *"Are you carrying?"*
"Yep, I Got a .45 in glove box, a 357 in the console & .32 in my ankle holster."
Cop; "Wow! What are you so afraid of?"

Grams; *"Not a damned thing!"*

"An old sheriff was attending an awards dinner; a lady commented; 'Sheriff, I see you have your pistol. Are you expecting trouble?' 'No Ma'am. If I were, I would'a brought my shotgun.'

"I was once asked by a lady visiting if I had gun in the house; "yes, I do."

'Well I hope it isn't loaded!'

'Of course! Guns can't work without bullets!'

'Are you that afraid of someone evil coming into your house?"

Nope. I'm not afraid of the house catching fire either, but I have four fire extinguishers and they're all loaded too!"

Average 911 response time; 5 minutes. Response time, .44 mag; 1400 fps.

From funny gun manual quotes;

"From my Kimber manual; "If a bullet is (lodged) in the bore, do not attempt to shoot it out by using another cartridge."

&

"Place the magazine... with the rounds facing forward."

&

"Firing: Place index finger on trigger, take aim and gently squeeze rearward until hammer is released and falls forward striking firing pin. Be prepared for loud noise and recoil. step 6. Continue procedure until magazine is empty and slide is locked open."

(so when the judge asks why you emptied a full mag into an intruder, tell him to RTFM)"

(And you thought manuals were useless!)

CH.
16 GUAGE

SNAPPY COMEBACKS

I ran across some zingers while doing this book. Couldn't bring myself to leave 'em out. Enjoy.

"How can you shoot those beautiful Doves?"

"You gotta lead 'em a lot, and remember to *follow through!*"

"How can you shoot such pretty deer?"

"I just shoot the ugly ones."

"How can you shoot wild animals?"

Same way you get to Carnegie Hall...
Practice, Practice, ***PRACTICE!***

"Why do you kill wild animals?"
"Ya gotta kill 'em before you can grill 'em!

"I'm against catch & release fishing!"
"Me too! That's why practice
CATCH, _EAT_ & RELEASE!"

"Guns cause crime!"
"Right, and spoons made YOU fat"

"Guns cause crime!"
"Then *MINE* must be DEFECTIVE!"

"GUNS CAUSE CRIME!"
"Gee, then Switzerland must have the
highest crime rate!"
(high-density guns per capita)

"NO GUNS, NO CRIME!"

"Then there's no crime in prisons!"

"I'M AFRAID OF GUNS"

"Me too, when they're held by CRIMINALS!"

"WITHOUT GUNS, THERE WOULDN'T BE ANY HIJACKED AIRPLANES"

"Did you forget about the *box cutters?*"

"WITHOUT GUNS, THERE WOULDN'T BE ANY CRIME"

"And without anti-gunners, there wouldn't be any stupidity."

"IT'S CRUEL TO KILL ANIMALS FOR FOOD"

"Go the store & ask for UN-killed meat."

"FARMERS ARE CRUEL TO ANIMALS."

"Don't talk with your mouth full!"

"I don't endorse killing animals."

"Then let all the rats, roaches
and flies reproduce."

**"I ONLY EAT MEAT RAISED IN STRESS-
FREE ENVIRONMENTS."**

"Where are stress-free places?
I'd like to live in one!"

FROM THE VEGANS' vacuuous skulls come
a few especially ludicrous catch phrases.

"I DON'T EAT ANYTHING WITH A FACE."

"I never eat animals with a **straight face.**
They taste so good, it makes me smile!"

"I'M A VEGAN; I CAN'T KILL ANIMALS."

"You're right about that;
it takes brains to hunt animals."

"I'M VEGAN"

"You descended from the
WORST HUNTERS!"

"HERBIVORES & VEGANS ARE SMARTER."

"They rank right up there with cows and sheep... *real Rhodes' Scholars!*"

"IT'S WRONG TO EAT ANYTHING FROM ANIMALS WITH FACES."

"Do shrimp & lobsters count?

No lips, no face, *no problem!*"

"VEGANS DON'T SUBSIDIZE KILLING "

"You must have a *SMART PLOW that* avoids moles, gophers, angleworms, snakes, fawns, quail & turkey chicks?"

"MANKIND HAS THE DENTITION OF AN HERBIVORE; ERGO, EATING ANIMALS IS CONTRARY TO EVOLUTION."

Actually, we have the teeth of the OMNIVORE, to eat meat when you get it, plants when you can't, and mud, moss & bugs when you're starving

**"WE RESEMBLE CHIMPS,
AND THEY DON'T EAT MEAT!"**

"WRONG AGAIN, CLYDE!"

"Wild chimps sometimes cannibalize other chimps. Ask any primatologist."

"It's WRONG TO EAT ANIMALS!"
"Then why did Got make 'em out of meat?"

"I LOVE ANIMALS!"
"Me too! Most are terrific,

with garlic & butter!"

"ANIMALS HAVE THEIR PLACE!"

"Right next to the mashed potatoes."

"You shoot innocent animals?"

"Nope, just the ones that look guilty."

"I'm against guns!"

"I respect your opinion; so I won't use my guns to protect you... Or your family."

"I don't think citizens should own guns."

"Neither did Hitler."

"YOU DON'T NEED A GUN;
THE COPS WILL PROTECT YOU!"

"911 response, ten minutes; my gun
responds at 1400 feet per second.

DO THE MATH!"

"YOU DON'T NEED A GUN;
THE COPS WILL PROTECT YOU!"

"Obviously, you've never been raped,
mugged or assaulted."

"I DON'T BELIEVE ANYONE SHOULD
OWN A GUN FOR SELF DEFENSE!"

"You'd rather be a dead victim
than a live hero?"

"I'M AGAINST GUNS!"

"GUNS won your freedom
to speak your mind, idiot."

"GUN OWNERS ARE BARBARIANS!"
"NO, we use guns
to keep barbarians *away!"*

"YOU DON'T NEED GUNS,
I DON'T CARE WHAT YOU SAY."

"ACTUALLY, THAT'S
WHY I NEED A GUN...
BECAUSE YOU *DON'T CARE"*

CH.
12 GUAGE

Humorous epitaphs

(from webpanda)...

"Here lies Lester Moore.
Four slugs
From a forty-four.
No Les
No More"
Boot Hill Cemetery, Tombstone, Arizona

"He was young
He was fair
But the Injuns
Raised his hair"
Colorado

"Bill Blake
Was hanged by mistake"
Boot Hill Cemetery, Tombstone, Arizona

"Here lays Butch.
We planted him raw.
He was quick on the trigger
But slow on the draw"
Silver City, Nevada

"Here lies a man named Zeke.
Second fastest draw in Cripple Creek"

Toothless Nell (Alice Chambers)
Killed 1876 in a Dance Hall brawl.
Her last words:
"Circumstances led me to this end."
Boot Hill Museum, Dodge City, Kansas

"Here lies the body of Arkansas Jim.
We made the mistake,

But the joke's on him"
Culver City

"He called
Bill Smith
A Liar"

Cripple Creek, CO

On the grave of a woman who died in 1984. Colorado Springs, Colorado. Her son, owner of Zeezo's Magic Castle in Colorado Springs, stated that his mother had been married to a Texan who is buried in Texas.

"I would
rather be here
than in Texas"

Salida, Colorado. On a hanged man

"Rab McBeth
Who died for the want
of another breath
1791-1823"

In a New Jersey cemetery Rebecca Freeland 1741

**"She drank good ale,
good punch and wine
And lived to the age of 99"**

On a grave digger

**"Hooray my brave boys
Lets rejoice at his fall
For if he had lived
He would have buried us all"**

**"And from the ONLY spam I ever liked,
the following seems appropriate"**

Watch your thoughts;
they become words.

Watch your words;
they become actions.

Watch your actions;
they become habits..

Watch your habits;
they become character.

Watch your character;
it becomes your destiny

APPENDIX 1

Somehow, I couldn't bring myself to end this book WITHOUT including the paperwork.

After all, we're up to our necks in paperwork whenever we buy a gun, so why not include the MOST IMPORTANT paperwork of all?

So, in case you don't already own a copy, allow me to lay one on you...

I give you;

the finest legal documentation to ever grace a sheet of velum... long may it prevail.

CH. 45-70

Documentation
for
WE the People...

"If liberty is worth keeping and free representative government worth saving, we must stand for all American fundamentals — not some, but all. All are woven into the great fabric of our national well-being. We cannot hold fast to some only, and abandon others that, for the moment, we find inconvenient. If one American fundamental is prostrated, others in the end will surely fall."

Albert J. Beveridge, (10/6/1862 – 4/27/1927)

Historian, US Senator

The founders collaborated, with the purest intention, the deepest passion and patriotism. Imagine the setting; you won a long and hard victory over a larger army equipped with better weapons and tactically-trained officers. You beat them with rag-tag colonialists, flintlocks and pitchforks. You won because of three things.

YOU had a taste of freedom and liked it.

Secondly, you tried to be heard, but the

government didn't listen.

Finally, You bore arms... *and RESISTED!*

And now it's time to build a better mousetrap. You're chosen to pen the Constitution. What words would you use? What powers shall you allocate? Most importantly, HOW do you ensure that your new government won't end up as rotten as the King's did?

Well, the framers did a *damned good job* of it. They used SIMPLE WORDS, not complex verbiage or legal-speak. Why did these educated men select such simple terms?

The Constitution was written for

We, the People.

Imagine how convoluted and obscure it would have been, had they caved to the temptation to write it in legal-speak, so ONLY the elite could understand it.

The biggest concepts are always expressed with the simplest words. God, freedom, arms, love, war; simple, eh?

The founders understood the vital role of heated debate, passionate disagreement and even the brutal sacrifices of armed revolution, with its ultimate reward, freedom from tyranny.

But nowadays we're seeing herds of sheep who would have our kids think in a politically correct way, much like George Orwell's "thought crimes" in 1984. Our ancestors would roll over in their graves! Where is it written that we must all agree? Who said we should support unpatriotic jerks like Obama, instead of critiquing every UN-American thing they do?

When did IMPEACHMENT become taboo?

A TRULY FREE SOCIETY ABHORS POLITICAL CORRECTNESS

A free society OPENLY scrutinizes its leaders. IT CULTIVATES diverse viewpoints. Vigorous dialogue is the difference between impeaching a president or serving a dictator.

Have a look at political cartoons from bygone eras; they'll curl your hair. The original reason for a free press was to attack our leaders with cartoons and scathing editorials, so everyone knew which politician was doing what, to whom. It went a long way towards keeping them honest. (don't laugh; at least they tried)

And yet, that tradition is now sadly lacking; when was the last time you saw a controversial political cartoon in a major newspaper? When did you last see a TV show that attacked the president's irrational, unconstitutional stance on a major issue? You don't; instead we see the major TV channels rush to support our president, as though ass-kissing were the main job of a free press.

We are losing our traditional American way. We are falling to the chaos-loving a-moralists, those sophomoric dolts in the left-controlled media who try to convince us that it's better to suffer together in mediocrity than to thrive in victory... OR that pacifism will somehow protect us from the barbarians at the gate.

Well, it's time for We the People to

Come OUT OF THE CLOSET!

It's time to go back

& read the documents.

I invite you to read the following chapters, to... See how far we have strayed from the original spirit of these incredible charters, some of the most beautiful, INSPIRED legal charters the world has ever seen.

THE DECLARATION

OF INDEPENDENCE

"When in the course of human events, it becomes necessary for one people to dissolve the political bands which have connected them with another, and to assume among the powers of the earth, the separate and equal station to which the Laws of Nature and of Nature's God entitle them, a decent respect to the opinions of mankind requires that they should declare the causes which impel them to the separation.

"We hold these truths to be self-evident, that all men are created equal, that they are endowed by their Creator with certain inalienable rights, that among these are life, liberty and the pursuit of happiness.

"That to secure these rights, governments are instituted among men, deriving their just powers from the consent of the governed. That whenever any form of government becomes destructive of these ends, it is the right of the people to alter or abolish it, and to institute new government, laying its foundation on such principles and organizing its powers in such form, as to them shall seem most likely to effect their safety and happiness.

"Prudence, indeed, will dictate that governments long established should not be changed for light and transient causes; and accordingly all experience hath shown, that mankind are more disposed to suffer, while evils are sufferable, than to right themselves by abolishing the forms to which they are accustomed.

But when a long train of abuses and usurpations, pursuing invariably the same object evinces a design to reduce them under absolute despotism, it is their right, it is their duty, to throw off such government, and to provide new guards for their future security.

Such has been the patient sufferance of these Colonies; and such is now the necessity which constrains them to alter their former systems of government. The history of the present King of Great Britain is a history of repeated injuries and usurpations, all having in direct object the establishment of an absolute tyranny over these States. To prove this, let facts be submitted to a candid world.

Charges

He has refused his Assent to Laws, the most wholesome and necessary for the public good.

He has forbidden his Governors to pass Laws of immediate and pressing importance, unless suspended in their operation till his Assent should be obtained; and when so suspended, he has utterly neglected to attend to them.

He has refused to pass other Laws for the accommodation of large districts of people, unless those people would relinquish the right of Representation in the Legislature, a right inestimable to them and formidable to tyrants only.

He has called together legislative bodies at places unusual, uncomfortable, and distant from the depository of their public Records, for the sole purpose of fatiguing them into compliance with his measures.

He has dissolved Representative Houses repeatedly, for opposing with manly firmness his invasions on the rights of the people.

He has refused for a long time, after such dissolutions, to cause others to be elected; whereby the Legislative powers, incapable of Annihilation, have returned to the People at large for their exercise; the State remaining in the mean time exposed to all the dangers of invasion from without, and convulsions within.

He has endeavoured to prevent the population of these States; for that purpose obstructing the Laws for Naturalization of Foreigners; refusing to pass others to encourage their migrations hither, and raising the conditions of new Appropriations of Lands.

He has obstructed the Administration of Justice, by refusing his Assent to Laws for establishing Judiciary powers.

He has made Judges dependent on his Will alone, for the tenure of their offices, and the amount and payment of their salaries.

He has erected a multitude of New Offices, and sent hither swarms of Officers to harrass our people, and eat out their substance.

He has kept among us, in times of peace, Standing Armies without the Consent of our legislatures.

He has affected to render the Military independent of and superior to the Civil power.

He has combined with others to subject us to a jurisdiction foreign to our constitution, and unacknowledged by our laws; giving his Assent to their Acts of pretended Legislation:

For Quartering large bodies of armed troops among us:

For protecting them, by a mock Trial, from punishment for any Murders which they should commit on the Inhabitants of these States:

For cutting off our Trade with all parts of the world:

For imposing Taxes on us without our Consent:

For depriving us in many cases, of the benefits of Trial by Jury:

For transporting us beyond Seas to be tried for pretended offences:

For abolishing the free System of English Laws in a neighbouring Province, establishing therein an Arbitrary government, and enlarging its Boundaries so as to render it at once an example and fit instrument for introducing the same absolute rule into these Colonies:

For taking away our Charters, abolishing our most valuable Laws, and altering fundamentally the Forms of our Governments:

For suspending our own Legislatures, and declaring themselves invested with power to legislate for us in all cases whatsoever.

He has abdicated Government here, by declaring us out of his Protection and waging War against us.

He has plundered our seas, ravaged our Coasts, burnt our towns, and destroyed the lives of our people.

He is at this time transporting large Armies of foreign Mercenaries to compleat the works of death, desolation and tyranny, already begun with circumstances of Cruelty & perfidy scarcely paralleled in the most barbarous ages, and totally unworthy the Head of a civilized nation.

He has constrained our fellow Citizens taken Captive on the high Seas to bear Arms against their Country, to become the executioners of their friends and Brethren, or to fall themselves by their Hands.

He has excited domestic insurrections amongst us, and has endeavoured to bring on the inhabitants of our frontiers, the merciless Indian Savages, whose known rule of warfare, is an undistinguished destruction of all ages, sexes and conditions.

CONCLUSION

In every stage of these Oppressions We have Petitioned for Redress in the most humble terms: Our repeated Petitions have been answered only by repeated injury. A Prince whose character is thus marked by every act which may define a Tyrant, is unfit to be the ruler of a free people.

Nor have We been wanting in attentions to our Brittish brethren.

We have warned them from time to time of attempts by their legislature to extend an unwarrantable jurisdiction over us.

We have reminded them of the circumstances of our emigration and settlement here. We have appealed to their native justice and magnanimity, and we have conjured them by the ties of our common kindred to disavow these usurpations, which, would inevitably interrupt our connections and correspondence.

They too have been deaf to the voice of justice and of consanguinity.

We must, therefore, acquiesce in the necessity, which denounces our Separation, and hold them, as we hold the rest of mankind, Enemies in War, in Peace Friends.

Summation

We, therefore, the Representatives of the united States of America, in General Congress, Assembled, appealing to the Supreme Judge of the world for the rectitude of our intentions, do, in the Name, and by Authority of the good People of these Colonies, solemnly publish and declare, That these United Colonies are, and of Right ought to be Free and Independent States; that they are Absolved from all Allegiance to the British Crown, and that all political connection between them and the State of Great Britain, is and ought to be totally dissolved; and that as Free and Independent States, they have full Power to levy War, conclude Peace, contract Alliances, establish Commerce, and to do all other Acts and Things which Independent States may of right do.

And for the support of this Declaration, with a firm reliance on the protection of divine Providence, we mutually pledge to each other our Lives, our Fortunes and our sacred Honor."

CH. 50 CAL

"THE CONSTITUTION OF THE UNITED STATES

We the People of the United States, in Order to form a more perfect Union, establish Justice, insure domestic Tranquility, provide for the common defence, promote the general Welfare, and secure the Blessings of Liberty to ourselves and our Posterity, do ordain and establish this Constitution for the United States of America.

Article I.
Congressional Provisions
All legislative Powers herein granted shall be vested in a Congress of the United States, which shall consist of a Senate and House of Representatives.

The House of Representatives shall be composed of Members chosen every second Year by the People of the several States, and the Electors in each State shall have the Qualifications requisite for Electors of the most numerous Branch of the State Legislature.

No Person shall be a Representative who shall not have attained to the Age of twenty five Years, and been seven Years a Citizen of the United States, and who shall not, when elected, be an Inhabitant of that State in which he shall be chosen. Representatives and direct Taxes shall be apportioned among the several States which may be included within this Union, according to their respective Numbers, which shall be determined by adding to the whole Number of free Persons, including those bound to Service for a Term of Years, and excluding Indians not taxed, three fifths of all other Persons.The actual Enumeration shall be made within three Years after the first Meeting of the Congress of the United States, and within every subsequent Term of ten Years, in such Manner as they shall by Law direct. The Number of Representatives shall not exceed one for every thirty Thousand, but each State shall have at Least one Representative; and until such enumeration shall be made, the State of New Hampshire shall be entitled to chuse three, Massachusetts eight, Rhode-Island and Providence Plantations one, Connecticut five, New-York six, New Jersey four, Pennsylvania eight, Delaware one, Maryland six, Virginia ten, North Carolina five, South Carolina five, and Georgia three. When vacancies happen in the Representation from any State, the Executive Authority thereof shall issue Writs of Election to fill such Vacancies. The House of Representatives shall chuse their Speaker and other Officers; and shall have the sole Power of Impeachment.

The Senate of the United States shall be composed of two Senators from each State, *chosen by the Legislature thereof*, and each Senator shall have one Vote.

Immediately after they shall be assembled in Consequence of the first Election, they shall be divided as equally as may be into three Classes. The Seats of the Senators of the first Class shall be vacated at the Expiration of the second Year, of the second Class at the Expiration of the fourth Year, and of the third Class at the Expiration of the sixth Year, so that one third may be chosen every second Year;and if Vacancies happen by Resignation, or otherwise, during the Recess of the Legislature of any State, the Executive thereof may make temporary Appointments until the next Meeting of the Legislature, which shall then fill such Vacancies.

No Person shall be a Senator who shall not have attained to the Age of thirty Years, and been nine Years a Citizen of the United States, and who shall not, when elected, be an Inhabitant of that State for which he shall be chosen.

The Vice President of the United States shall be President of the Senate, but shall have no Vote, unless they be equally divided. The Senate shall chuse their other Officers, and also a President pro tempore, in the Absence of the Vice President, or when he shall exercise the Office of President of the United States.
The Senate shall have the sole Power to try all Impeachments. When sitting for that Purpose, they shall be on Oath or Affirmation. When the President of the United States is tried, the Chief Justice shall preside: And no Person shall be convicted without the Concurrence of two thirds of the Members present.
Judgment in Cases of Impeachment shall not extend further than to removal from Office, and disqualification to hold and enjoy any Office of

honor, Trust or Profit under the United States: but the Party convicted shall nevertheless be liable and subject to Indictment, Trial, Judgment and Punishment, according to Law.

The Times, Places and Manner of holding Elections for Senators and Representatives, shall be prescribed in each State by the Legislature thereof; but the Congress may at any time by Law make or alter such Regulations, except as to the Places of chusing Senators.
The Congress shall assemble at least once in every Year, and such Meeting shall be on the first Monday in December unless they shall by Law appoint a different Day.

Each House shall be the Judge of the Elections, Returns and Qualifications of its own Members, and a Majority of each shall constitute a Quorum to do Business; but a smaller Number may adjourn from day to day, and may be authorized to compel the Attendance of absent Members, in such Manner, and under such Penalties as each House may provide.
Each House may determine the Rules of its Proceedings, punish its Members for disorderly Behaviour, and, with the Concurrence of two thirds, expel a Member.
Each House shall keep a Journal of its Proceedings, and from time to time publish the same, excepting such Parts as may in their Judgment require Secrecy; and the Yeas and Nays of the Members of either House on any question shall, at the Desire of one fifth of those Present, be entered on the Journal.
Neither House, during the Session of Congress, shall, without the Consent of the other, adjourn for more than three days, nor to any other Place than that in which the two Houses shall be sitting.

The Senators and Representatives shall receive a Compensation for their Services, to be ascertained by Law, and paid out of the Treasury of the United States. They shall in all Cases, except Treason, Felony and Breach of the Peace, be privileged from Arrest during their Attendance at the Session of their respective Houses, and in going to and returning from the same; and for any Speech or Debate in either House, they shall not be questioned in any other Place.

No Senator or Representative shall, during the Time for which he was elected, be appointed to any civil Office under the Authority of the United States, which shall have been created, or the Emoluments whereof shall have been encreased during such time; and no Person holding any Office under the United States, shall be a Member of either House during his Continuance in Office.

All Bills for raising Revenue shall originate in the House of Representatives; but the Senate may propose or concur with Amendments as on other Bills.

Every Bill which shall have passed the House of Representatives and the Senate, shall, before it become a Law, be presented to the President of the United States: If he approve he shall sign it, but if not he shall return it, with his Objections to that House in which it shall have originated, who shall enter the Objections at large on their Journal, and proceed to reconsider it. If after such Reconsideration two thirds of that House shall agree to pass the Bill, it shall be sent, together with the Objections, to the other House, by which it shall likewise be reconsidered, and if approved by two thirds of that House, it shall become a Law. But in all such Cases the Votes of both Houses shall be determined by yeas and Nays, and the Names of the Persons voting for and against the Bill shall be entered on the Journal of each House respectively. If any Bill shall not be returned by the President within ten Days (Sundays excepted) after it shall have been presented to him, the Same shall be a Law, in like Manner as if he had signed it, unless the Congress by their Adjournment prevent its Return, in which Case it shall not be a Law. Every Order, Resolution, or Vote to which the Concurrence of the Senate and House of Representatives may be necessary (except on a question of Adjournment) shall be presented to the President of the United States; and before the Same shall take Effect, shall be approved by him, or being disapproved by him, shall be repassed by two thirds of the Senate and House of Representatives, according to the Rules and Limitations prescribed in the Case of a Bill.

The Congress shall have Power to lay and collect Taxes, Duties, Imposts and Excises, to pay the Debts and provide for the common Defence and general Welfare of the United States; but all Duties, Imposts and Excises shall be uniform throughout the United States;
To borrow Money on the credit of the United States;
To regulate Commerce with foreign Nations, and among the several States, and with the Indian Tribes;
To establish an uniform Rule of Naturalization, and uniform Laws on the subject of Bankruptcies throughout the United States;
To coin Money, regulate the Value thereof, and of foreign Coin, and fix the Standard of Weights and Measures;
To provide for the Punishment of counterfeiting the Securities and current Coin of the United States;
To establish Post Offices and post Roads;
To promote the Progress of Science and useful

Arts, by securing for limited Times to Authors and Inventors the exclusive Right to their respective Writings and Discoveries;

To constitute Tribunals inferior to the supreme Court;

To define and punish Piracies and Felonies committed on the high Seas, and Offences against the Law of Nations; To declare War, grant Letters of Marque and Reprisal, and make Rules concerning Captures on Land and Water;

To raise and support Armies, but no Appropriation of Money to that Use shall be for a longer Term than two Years;

To provide and maintain a Navy;

To make Rules for the Government and Regulation of the land and naval Forces;

To provide for calling forth the Militia to execute the Laws of the Union, suppress Insurrections and repel Invasions;

To provide for organizing, arming, and disciplining, the Militia, and for governing such Part of them as may be employed in the Service of the United States, reserving to the States respectively, the Appointment of the Officers, and the Authority of training the Militia according to the discipline prescribed by Congress;

To exercise exclusive Legislation in all Cases whatsoever, over such District (not exceeding ten Miles square) as may, by Cession of particular States, and the Acceptance of Congress, become the Seat of the Government of the United States, and to exercise like Authority over all Places purchased by the Consent of the Legislature of the State in which the Same shall be, for the Erection of Forts, Magazines, Arsenals, dock-Yards, and other needful Buildings; --And To make all Laws which shall be necessary and proper for carrying into Execution the foregoing Powers, and all other Powers vested by this Constitution in the

Government of the United States, or in any Department or Officer thereof.

The Migration or Importation of such Persons as any of the States now existing shall think proper to admit, shall not be prohibited by the Congress prior to the Year one thousand eight hundred and eight, but a Tax or duty may be imposed on such Importation, not exceeding ten dollars for each Person.
The Privilege of the Writ of Habeas Corpus shall not be suspended, unless when in Cases of Rebellion or Invasion the public Safety may require it. No Bill of Attainder or ex post facto Law shall be passed.

No Capitation, or other direct, Tax shall be laid, unless in Proportion to the Census or Enumeration herein before directed to be taken.
No Tax or Duty shall be laid on Articles exported from any State.
No Preference shall be given by any Regulation of Commerce or Revenue to the Ports of one State over those of another; nor shall Vessels bound to, or from, one State, be obliged to enter, clear, or pay Duties in another.

No Money shall be drawn from the Treasury, but in Consequence of Appropriations made by Law; and a regular Statement and Account of the Receipts and Expenditures of all public Money shall be published from time to time.

No Title of Nobility shall be granted by the United States: And no Person holding any Office of Profit or Trust under them, shall, without the Consent of the Congress, accept of any present, Emolument, Office, or Title, of any kind whatever, from any King, Prince, or foreign State.

No State shall enter into any Treaty, Alliance, or Confederation; grant Letters of Marque and Reprisal; coin Money; emit Bills of Credit; make any Thing but gold and silver Coin a Tender in Payment of Debts; pass any Bill of Attainder, ex post facto Law, or Law impairing the Obligation of Contracts, or grant any Title of Nobility.

No State shall, without the Consent of the Congress, lay any Imposts or Duties on Imports or Exports, except what may be absolutely necessary for executing it's inspection Laws; and the net Produce of all Duties and Imposts, laid by any State on Imports or Exports, shall be for the Use of the Treasury of the United States; and all such Laws shall be subject to the Revision and Controul of the Congress.
No State shall, without the Consent of Congress, lay any Duty of Tonnage, keep Troops, or Ships of War in time of Peace, enter into any Agreement or Compact with another State, or with a foreign Power, or engage in War, unless actually invaded, or in such imminent Danger as will not admit of delay.

Executive powers

The executive Power shall be vested in a President of the United States of America. He shall hold his Office during the Term of four Years, and, together with the Vice President, chosen for the same Term, be elected, as follows:

Each State shall appoint, in such Manner as the Legislature thereof may direct, a Number of Electors, equal to the whole Number of Senators and Representatives to which the State may be entitled in the Congress: but no Senator or Representative, or Person holding an Office of

Trust or Profit under the United States, shall be appointed an Elector.

The Electors shall meet in their respective States, and vote by Ballot for two Persons, of whom one at least shall not be an Inhabitant of the same State with themselves. And they shall make a List of all the Persons voted for, and of the Number of Votes for each; which List they shall sign and certify, and transmit sealed to the Seat of the Government of the United States, directed to the President of the Senate. The President of the Senate shall, in the Presence of the Senate and House of Representatives, open all the Certificates, and the Votes shall then be counted. The Person having the greatest Number of Votes shall be the President, if such Number be a Majority of the whole Number of Electors appointed; and if there be more than one who have such Majority, and have an equal Number of Votes, then the House of Representatives shall immediately chuse by Ballot one of them for President; and if no Person have a Majority, then from the five highest on the List the said House shall in like Manner chuse the President. But in chusing the President, the Votes shall be taken by States, the Representation from each State having one Vote; a quorum for this Purpose shall consist of a Member or Members from two thirds of the States, and a Majority of all the States shall be necessary to a Choice. In every Case, after the Choice of the President, the Person having the greatest Number of Votes of the Electors shall be the Vice President. But if there should remain two or more who have equal Votes, the Senate shall chuse from them by Ballot the Vice President

The Congress may determine the Time of chusing the Electors, and the Day on which they shall give their Votes; which Day shall be the same throughout the United States.

No Person except a natural born Citizen, or a Citizen of the United States, at the time of the Adoption of this Constitution, shall be eligible to the Office of President; neither shall any Person be eligible to that Office who shall not have attained to the Age of thirty five Years, and been fourteen Years a Resident within the United States.

In Case of the Removal of the President from Office, or of his Death, Resignation, or Inability to discharge the Powers and Duties of the said Office, the Same shall devolve on the Vice President, and the Congress may by Law provide for the Case of Removal, Death, Resignation or Inability, both of the President and Vice President, declaring what Officer shall then act as President, and such Officer shall act accordingly, until the Disability be removed, or a President shall be elected.

The President shall, at stated Times, receive for his Services, a Compensation, which shall neither be increased nor diminished during the Period for which he shall have been elected, and he shall not receive within that Period any other Emolument from the United States, or any of them.

Before he enter on the Execution of his Office, he shall take the following Oath or Affirmation:--"I do solemnly swear (or affirm) that I will faithfully execute the Office of President of the United States, and will to the best of my Ability, preserve, protect and defend the Constitution of the United States."

The President shall be Commander in Chief of the Army and Navy of the United States, and of the Militia of the several States, when called into the actual Service of the United States; he may require the Opinion, in writing, of the principal Officer in each of the executive Departments, upon any Subject relating to the Duties of their respective Offices, and he shall have Power to grant Reprieves and Pardons for Offences against the United States, except in Cases of Impeachment.

He shall have Power, by and with the Advice and Consent of the Senate, to make Treaties, provided two thirds of the Senators present concur; and he shall nominate, and by and with the Advice and Consent of the Senate, shall appoint Ambassadors, other public Ministers and Consuls, Judges of the supreme Court, and all other Officers of the United States, whose Appointments are not herein otherwise provided for, and which shall be established by Law: but the Congress may by Law vest the Appointment of such inferior Officers, as they think proper, in the President alone, in the Courts of Law, or in the Heads of Departments. The President shall have Power to fill up all Vacancies that may happen during the Recess of the Senate, by granting Commissions which shall expire at the End of their next Session.

He shall from time to time give to the Congress Information of the State of the Union, and recommend to their Consideration such Measures as he shall judge necessary and expedient; he may, on extraordinary Occasions, convene both Houses, or either of them, and in Case of Disagreement between them, with Respect to the Time of Adjournment, he may adjourn them to such Time as he shall think proper; he shall receive Ambassadors and other public Ministers; he shall take Care that the Laws be faithfully executed, and shall Commission all the Officers of the United States.

The President, Vice President and all civil Officers of the United States, shall be removed from Office on Impeachment for, and Conviction of, Treason, Bribery, or other high Crimes and Misdemeanors.

Article. III.
Judicial Powers

The judicial Power of the United States shall be vested in one supreme Court, and in such inferior Courts as the Congress may from time to time ordain and establish. The Judges, both of the supreme and inferior Courts, shall hold their Offices during good Behaviour, and shall, at stated Times, receive for their Services a Compensation, which shall not be diminished during their Continuance in Office.

The judicial Power shall extend to all Cases, in Law and Equity, arising under this Constitution, the Laws of the United States, and Treaties made, or which shall be made, under their Authority; --to all Cases affecting Ambassadors, other public Ministers and Consuls; --to all Cases of admiralty and maritime Jurisdiction; --to Controversies to which the United States shall be a Party; --to Controversies between two or more States; --between a State and Citizens of another State --between Citizens of different States; --between Citizens of the same State claiming Lands under Grants of different States, and between a State, or the Citizens thereof, and foreign States, Citizens or Subjects.

In all Cases affecting Ambassadors, other public Ministers and Consuls, and those in which a State shall be Party, the supreme Court shall have original Jurisdiction. In all the other Cases before mentioned, the supreme Court shall have appellate Jurisdiction, both as to Law and Fact, with such Exceptions, and under such Regulations as the Congress shall make. The Trial of all Crimes, except in Cases of Impeachment, shall be by Jury; and such Trial shall be held in the State where the said Crimes shall have been committed; but when not committed within any State, the Trial shall be at such Place or Places as the Congress may by Law have directed.

Treason against the United States shall consist only in levying War against them, or in adhering to their Enemies, giving them Aid and Comfort. No Person shall be convicted of Treason unless on the Testimony of two Witnesses to the same overt Act, or on Confession in open Court. The Congress shall have Power to declare the Punishment of Treason, but no Attainder of Treason shall work Corruption of Blood, or Forfeiture except during the Life of the Person attained

Article. IV.
State Protections

Full Faith and Credit shall be given in each State to the public Acts, Records, and judicial Proceedings of every other State. And the Congress may by general Laws prescribe the Manner in which such Acts, Records and Proceedings shall be proved, and the Effect thereof.

The Citizens of each State shall be entitled to all Privileges and Immunities of Citizens in the several States. A Person charged in any State with Treason, Felony, or other Crime, who shall flee from Justice, and be found in another State, shall on Demand of the executive Authority of the State from which he fled, be delivered up, to be removed to the State having Jurisdiction of the Crime. *No Person held to Service or Labour in one State, under the Laws thereof, escaping into another, shall, in Consequence of any Law or Regulation therein, be discharged from such Service or Labour, but shall be delivered up on Claim of the Party to whom such Service or Labour may be due.*

New States may be admitted by the Congress into this Union; but no new State shall be formed or erected within the Jurisdiction of any other State; nor any State be formed by the Junction of two or more States, or Parts of States, without the Consent of the Legislatures of the States concerned as well as of the Congress.

The Congress shall have Power to dispose of and make all needful Rules and Regulations respecting the Territory or other Property belonging to the United States; and nothing in this Constitution shall be so construed as to Prejudice any Claims of the United States, or of any particular State.

The United States shall guarantee to every State in this Union a Republican Form of Government, and shall protect each of them against Invasion; and on Application of the Legislature, or of the Executive (when the Legislature cannot be convened), against domestic Violence.

Articles V-VII
Procedures for Amendments

The Congress, whenever two thirds of both Houses shall deem it necessary, shall propose Amendments to this Constitution, or, on the Application of the Legislatures of two thirds of the several States, shall call a Convention for proposing

Amendments, which, in either Case, shall be valid to all Intents and Purposes, as Part of this Constitution, when ratified by the Legislatures of three fourths of the several States, or by Conventions in three fourths thereof, as the one or the other Mode of Ratification may be proposed by the Congress; Provided that no Amendment which may be made prior to the Year One thousand eight hundred and eight shall in any Manner affect the first and fourth Clauses in the Ninth Section of the first Article; and that no State, without its Consent, shall be deprived of its equal Suffrage in the Senate.

All Debts contracted and Engagements entered into, before the Adoption of this Constitution, shall be as valid against the United States under this Constitution, as under the Confederation.

This Constitution, and the Laws of the United States which shall be made in Pursuance thereof; and all Treaties made, or which shall be made, under the Authority of the United States, shall be the supreme Law of the Land; and the Judges in every State shall be bound thereby, any Thing in the Constitution or Laws of any State to the Contrary notwithstanding.

The Senators and Representatives before mentioned, and the Members of the several State Legislatures, and all executive and judicial Officers, both of the United States and of the several States, shall be bound by Oath or Affirmation, to support this Constitution; but no religious Test shall ever be required as a Qualification to any Office or public Trust under the United States.

The Ratification of the Conventions of nine States, shall be sufficient for the Establishment of this Constitution between the States so ratifying the Same.

Attest William Jackson
Secretary done in Convention by the Unanimous
Consent of the States present the Seventeenth Day
of September in the Year of our Lord one thousand
seven hundred and E ighty seven and of the
Independence of the United States of America the
Twelfth In witness whereof We have hereunto
subscribed   our   Names,Go.   WASHINGTON--
Presidt.
and deputy from Virginia

New Hampshire
JOHN LANGDON
NICHOLAS GILMAN
Massachusetts
NATHANIEL GORHAM
RUFUS KING
Connecticut
WM. SAML. JOHNSON
ROGER SHERMAN
New York . . . .
ALEXANDER HAMILTON New Jersey
WIL: LIVINGSTON
DAVID BREARLEY.
WM. PATERSON.
JONA: DAYTON
Pennsylvania
B FRANKLIN
THOMAS MIFFLIN
ROBT MORRIS
GEO. CLYMER
THOS. FITZ SIMONS
JARED INGERSOLL
JAMES WILSON
GOUV MORRIS
Delaware
GEO: READ
GUNNING BEDFORD jun
JOHN DICKINSON

RICHARD BASSETT
JACO: BROOM
Maryland
JAMES MCHENRY
DAN OF ST THOS. JENIFER
DANL CARROLL
Virginia
JOHN BLAIR
JAMES MADISON
North Carolina
WM. BLOUNT
RICHD. DOBBS SPAIGHT
HU WILLIAMSON
J. RUTLEDGE
South Carolina
CHARLES COTESWORTH PINCKNEY
CHARLES PINCKNEY
PIERCE BUTLER
Georgia
WILLIAM FEW
ABR BALDWIN

In Convention Monday, September 17th, 1787. Present The States of New Hampshire, Massachusetts, Connecticut, Mr. Hamilton from New York, New Jersey, Pennsylvania, Delaware, Maryland, Virginia, North Carolina, South Carolina and Georgia.Resolved, That the preceeding Constitution be laid before the United States in Congress assembled, and that it is the Opinion of this Convention, that it should afterwards be submitted to a Convention of Delegates, chosen in each State by the People thereof, under the Recommendation of its Legislature, for their Assent and Ratification; and that each Convention assenting to, and ratifying the Same, should give Notice thereof to the United States in Congress assembled. Resolved, That it is the Opinion of this Convention, that as soon as the Conventions of nine States shall have ratified this Constitution, the United States in Congress assembled should fix a Day on which Electors should be appointed by the States which have ratified the same, and a Day on which the Electors should assemble to vote for the President, and the Time and Place for commencing Proceedings under this Constitution. That after such Publication the Electors should be appointed, and the Senators and Representatives elected: That the Electors should meet on the Day fixed for the Election of the President, and should transmit their Votes certified, signed, sealed and directed, as the Constitution requires, to the Secretary of the United States in Congress assembled, that the Senators and Representatives should convene at the Time and Place assigned; that the Senators should appoint a President of the Senate, for the sole purpose of receiving, opening and counting the Votes for President; and, that after he shall be chosen, the Congress, together with the President, should, without Delay, proceed to execute this Constitution.By the Unanimous Order of the Convention

Go. WASHINGTON--Presidt.
W. JACKSON Secretary.

CH. 54

Bill of Rights

The Bill of Rights: A Transcription
The Preamble to The Bill of Rights

"Congress of the United States begun and held at the City of New-York, on Wednesday the fourth of March, one thousand seven hundred and eighty nine.

THE Conventions of a number of the States, having at the time of their adopting the Constitution, expressed a desire, in order to prevent misconstruction or abuse of its powers, that further declaratory and restrictive clauses should be added: And as extending the ground of public confidence in the Government, will best ensure the beneficent ends of its institution.

RESOLVED by the Senate and House of Representatives of the United States of America, in Congress assembled, two thirds of both Houses concurring, that the following Articles be proposed to the Legislatures of the several States, as amendments to the Constitution of the United States, all, or any of which Articles, when ratified by three fourths of the said Legislatures, to be valid to all intents and purposes, as part of the said Constitution; viz.

ARTICLES in addition to, and Amendment of the Constitution of the United States of America, proposed by Congress, and ratified by the Legislatures of the several States, pursuant to the fifth Article of the original Constitution.

(Note: The following text is a transcription of the first ten amendments to the Constitution in their original form. These amendments were ratified December 15, 1791, and form what is known as the "Bill of Rights.")

Amendment I

Congress shall make no law respecting an establishment of religion, or prohibiting the free exercise thereof; or abridging the freedom of speech, or of the press; or the right of the people peaceably to assemble, and to petition the Government for a redress of grievances.

Amendment II

A well regulated Militia, being necessary to the security of a free State, the right of the people to keep and bear Arms, shall not be infringed.

Amendment III

No Soldier shall, in time of peace be quartered in any house, without the consent of the Owner, nor in time of war, but in a manner to be prescribed by law.

Amendment IV

The right of the people to be secure in their persons, houses, papers, and effects, against unreasonable searches and seizures, shall not be violated, and no Warrants shall issue, but upon probable cause, supported by Oath or affirmation, and particularly describing the place to be searched, and the persons or things to be seized.

Amendment V

No person shall be held to answer for a capital, or otherwise infamous crime, unless on a presentment or indictment of a Grand Jury, except in cases arising in the land or naval forces, or in the Militia, when in actual service in time of War or public danger; nor shall any person be subject for the same offence to be twice put in jeopardy of life or limb; nor shall be compelled in any criminal case to be a witness against himself, nor be deprived of life, liberty, or property, without due process of law; nor shall private property be taken for public use, without just compensation.

Amendment VI

In all criminal prosecutions, the accused shall enjoy the right to a speedy and public trial, by an impartial jury of the State and district wherein the crime shall have been committed, which district shall have been previously ascertained by law, and to be informed of the nature and cause of the accusation; to be confronted with the witnesses against him; to have compulsory process for obtaining witnesses in his favor, and to have the Assistance of Counsel for his defence.

Amendment VII

In Suits at common law, where the value in controversy shall exceed twenty dollars, the right of trial by jury shall be preserved, and no fact tried by a jury, shall be otherwise re-examined in any Court of the United States, than according to the rules of the common law.

Amendment VIII

Excessive bail shall not be required, nor excessive fines imposed, nor cruel and unusual punishments inflicted.

Amendment IX

The enumeration in the Constitution, of certain rights, shall not be construed to deny or disparage others retained by the people.

Amendment X

The powers not delegated to the United States by the Constitution, nor prohibited by it to the States, are reserved to the States respectively, or to the people."

I didn't bother to print the remaining amendments. I'd rather mention things more to my point.

The four words most dangerous to

freedom lovers...

"IT CAN'T HAPPEN HERE!"

It's time to wake up and smell the coffee!

Our biggest Achilles tendon is that we refuse to believe that we could lose our guns. We can no longer afford to be so smug and lazy. There are people who are totally focused on taking our guns, just as there were folks who hated alcohol.

.

Remember, _WE HAD GUNS_

when we repealed Prohibition.

OR... WE'D *STILL BE DRY!*

Sure, we got our booze back, but only because damn near everyone in America wanted alcohol. Now be honest; how many people would fight that hard so you and I can keep our guns?

There are no Mulligans in Congress. The Federal government has demonstrated it many times; power lost to the Feds never gets returned. The government is a huge, sticky-armed octopus.

Remember that all it takes is a consensus shift in the way guns are perceived by the masses, many of whom have recently entered our Country from countries that already had corrupt federal governments and total gun control. They are already accustomed to having no freedom, and as long as the proposed bills don't cut their welfare checks they just don't give a damn about us or keeping our rifles.

The ignorant masses are growing in number. I wish they weren't, but wishes don't keep our guns safe. ONLY action can do that.

It's time to up the ante, folks, while we still have some chips in front of us.

The end (?)

I hope you enjoyed my book. If it helps just a few folks to see behind the smoke and mirrors of the gun-grabbers' insane arguments, it will be well worth the effort. Defending our way of life is never easy, but it IS simple... It just takes the same things as always.

I'm talkin' about
the three G'S...

God

Guns

&

Guts

Amen.

www.ingramcontent.com/pod-product-compliance
Lightning Source LLC
Chambersburg PA
CBHW070105290526
45789CB00005B/1931